22-50 Ncm

Lloyds Bank Annual Review

To Fred Hirsch

Lloyds Bank Annual Review

The Market on Trial

Volume 2

Edited by
Christopher Johnson

 Pinter Publishers, London and New York

First published in Great Britain in 1989 by
Pinter Publishers Limited
25 Floral Street, London WC2E 9DS

British Library Cataloguing in Publication Data

A CIP catalogue record for this book is available from the
British Library
ISBN 0-86187-704-7
ISSN 9053-5004

Library of Congress Cataloging-in-Publication Data

CIP Data available from the Library of Congress

Typeset by Mayhew Typesetting, Bristol, England
Printed and bound in Great Britain by
Biddles Ltd, Guildford and King's Lynn

Contents

Introduction

Christopher Johnson

Last year the first volume of *Lloyds Bank Annual Review*, which succeeded the quarterly *Lloyds Bank Review*, was entitled *Privatization and Ownership*. It brought together some 'classic' articles published in previous quarterly issues of the *Review* and a number of original contributions. This year, the second volume broadens out from that base to cover the wider, but related, theme of *The Market on Trial*. Privatization in the United Kingdom and elsewhere has been one way of enhancing the role of market forces in the economy, but there are many others, which are discussed here.

We are fortunate in having the agreement of the Fred Hirsch Memorial Trust to reprint the Fred Hirsch Memorial Lectures, given by seven distinguished economists over the decade 1978–87. All but one of the lectures were first printed in the quarterly *Lloyds Bank Review*. They are accompanied by three additional essays; the Institute of Economic Affairs lecture by Nigel Lawson, the Chancellor of the Exchequer; the Fulvio Guerrini lecture by Professor Sir Alan Peacock; and an appreciation of the importance of the late Fred Hirsch as an economic thinker by Peter Oppenheimer. We also express our gratitude to them for permission to print their contributions. This introduction tries to make a general statement on the theme of the book.

The Market on Trial is a play on words. Market solutions are being tried out in many areas of activity and in many countries where they were until recently excluded by the prevailing political consensus. Markets themselves, even where they have been operating for a long time, are also being critically judged on their performance; witness 'Black Monday' in world stock markets in October 1987. It is important, therefore, to assess what markets should or should not be expected to do. 'The market' also has a double meaning, referring both to a certain macroeconomic form of organization, and to specific microsectors within it.

No economy either gives complete sway to free market mechanisms or totally excludes them. The degree to which any particular economy is a free market economy can be defined by the scope of state involvement, either directly by ownership, or indirectly by regulation, in markets for particular

Christopher Johnson is Chief Economic Adviser, Lloyds Bank.

products and services. Even where there is a low level of state ownership, there may be a high level of state regulation, as in the Federal Republic of Germany, for example. The degree of freedom of each service or product market may be defined by examining not only the state's ownership or regulatory roles in it, but also the extent to which freedom of entry and operation is circumscribed by anti-competitive behaviour on the part of the market participants themselves. We quickly reach the paradox by which the state may have to intervene in the market to restore competition and thus force it to be free.

State intervention in markets is usually seen in terms of public ownership of business or public provision of services, and the debate about its scope is then the standard political clash of left against right. Advocates of the free market generally concede that the state has a duty to 'hold the ring' by means of suitable legislation and regulation. The way in which this is done, however, makes a big difference to the degree of indirect state influence on the market, and to the amount of freedom enjoyed by participants. Regulation has in fact become one apex of a triangle, in which the other two are state ownership and market freedom. Regulation can be as much an alternative to market freedom as is state ownership, for example in the privatization of the state monopolies of the UK. The regulator may have as much power, and as little valid basis, for imposing prices on a non-competitive industry as has the state planner.

The Thatcher government has correctly perceived that the introduction of market forces is to do with not only substituting the private for the public sector in many areas, but also deregulating parts of the private sector which have been held back by excessive regulation, see Lawson (p. 28). However, it has been necessary to bring in new structures of regulation to offset the danger of substituting private for public monopoly in the public corporations, such as gas and electricity. What cannot be directly ruled has to be indirectly regulated. The courts will come to play a more important role in such cases. They are as much an organ of the state as ministers or civil servants, if a more unpredictable and independent one.

The discussion of markets in these essays often focuses on particular markets which give cause for concern, such as those for labour, money, stocks and shares, foreign exchange, commodities and housing. If one important market goes wrong, many other markets may suffer by contagion. Yet there is little general agreement on which of these key markets should be free, which should be controlled, and how they should be regulated. One kind of free marketeer may believe in a controlled money market combined with a free labour market, another in a controlled foreign exchange market combined with a free money market. Some of the discussion is also in general terms about the free market economic system, and goes back to Adam Smith.

It is worth quoting the passage in *The Wealth of Nations* which dominates arguments about the market:

But the annual revenue of every society is always precisely equal to the exchangeable value of the whole annual produce of its industry, or is precisely the same thing with that exchangeable value. As every individual, therefore, endeavours as much as he can both to employ his capital in the support of domestick industry, and so to direct that industry that its produce may be of the greatest value; every individual necessarily labours to render the annual revenue of the society as great as he can. He generally, indeed, neither intends to promote the public interest, nor knows how much he is promoting it. By preferring the support of domestick industry to that of foreign industry, he intends only his own security; and by directing that industry in such a manner as its produce may be of the greatest value, he intends only his own gain, and he is in this, as in many other cases, led by an invisible hand to promote an end which was not part of his intention.[1]

A superstructure of interpretation has been erected on this simple proposition. It is often claimed that Smith was arguing that individual self-interest is the best way in which to maximise social welfare. Welfare economists have in their turn cast doubt on this theorem as at best a special case which is seldom exemplified in practice. However, Smith seems to us to be propounding a self-evident statistical truth. He begins by stating the analytical equivalence of what we would call the output, income and expenditure concepts of gross domestic product. Taking it as axiomatic that it is an objective of public policy to maximize GDP, and that the whole is the sum of its parts, he then easily demonstrates that public policy is served if each individual maximizes his own output, thus contributing to a rise in the national income.

Smith does not appear to be saying that individual self-interest contributes to other goals of public policy, such as fair distribution of income, nor does he, in this passage at any rate, address the question whether maximum individual effort is the most efficient form of industrial organization. The invisible hand turns out to amount to no more than the law of large numbers. Each individual's output is too small to make a perceptible difference to national income, but every individual's output taken together is simply what the national income is. (There is a somewhat mercantilist aside about preferring domestic industry, but, as Smith was anything but a mercantilist, we will let it pass as a statistical observation about the difference between gross *domestic* output and gross *national* output.)

Even if Smith did not mean what some of his interpreters have read into him, we should still consider seriously what the free marketeers are arguing, as outlined in Hahn's critical appraisal (p. 86). First, decentralized economic decision-making by individuals is better than centralized control by bureaucrats, even if the consequences of their actions for society were not specifically intended. This can be an argument about the merits of economic freedom — working for yourself and not someone else — as a welfare benefit in its own right, even at the cost of some sacrifice in total

GDP. Peacock emphasizes this merit of the market, and proposes profit-sharing to overcome the alienation of workers from employers (p. 47). There can also be a stronger claim that productive efficiency is increased by decentralized industrial structure. Smith certainly believed that monopolies and restrictive practices were a conspiracy against the public interest, and his theory of the merits of the division of labour should not be twisted into a defence of monopoly on the grounds that it facilitates economies of scale.

Decentralization has not been a notable feature of the free market approach by British ministers since 1979. Central government power has been greatly increased at the expense of local authorities, particularly in the field of education. South-East England and neighbouring regions have increased their predominance in the economy, at the expense of the North, Wales and Scotland. Monopolies and mergers policy is vacillating and lacking in clear rationale, and plans to take more vigorous action to tackle price-fixing agreements have taken years to reach even the discussion stage. Action has been taken to reduce the amount of regulation faced by small firms, but it has not had a notable impact.

The need to preserve freedom of competition has not been sufficiently recognized by advocates of the free market. It has been argued that the European internal market to be created by 1992 will install competition over a wider area so that companies which might be dominant in the UK market alone will be subject to competition in the European market. This argument presupposes that barriers will in fact be removed, which may take time, and that divergent national tastes will disappear, which may take even longer. The Institute of Economic Affairs, which is known for its advocacy of the free market, has always stressed the need for more competition in UK markets. A higher rate of inflation than in other major industrial countries persists in the UK partly because British companies are more willing and able than some of their rivals to accept relatively high unit labour-cost increases and pass them on in the form of higher prices.

The other main defect of the free market is its external diseconomies in the shape of pollution, in such forms as the disfigurement of the environment, the failure to control toxic wastes, and dangers to the health and safety of employees and the public. It is too easy to retort that such matters are dealt with by regulation. Regulations may not be sufficiently strict, and there are seldom enough inspection staff in the UK to see that they are enforced. Regulation also needs to cover industrial processes themselves, rather than only their results. While excessive regulation may be a constraint on industry, inadequate regulation is a burden on society.

We shall examine some of the major markets covered by the lectures, and try to assess them according to the usual criteria. First, does the price mechanism bring about equilibrium between supply and demand; or is there a disequilibrium, with excess demand or excess supply? Second, is it a free market, in the sense that both freedom of entry and freedom to buy and sell are unhindered by restrictions imposed by existing market participants? Third, is it a private market, in the sense that the public sector does not distort its functioning either by direct participation, or indirectly by regulation? Fourth, is it an efficient market in terms of production, in that it maximizes the rate of growth of the good or service being bought and sold, without external costs to economic welfare? Fifth, is it an efficient market in terms of allocation, in that it results in prices which encourage the optimum use of scarce resources? Sixth, is it a fair market, resulting in a socially acceptable pattern of distribution among participants? And finally, is it a stable market, in which price variations are continuous, and take into account fundamental economic factors, as well as volatile short-term fads? Clearly not all of these criteria can be satisfied at once, and markets and economies in the real world are only imperfect realizations of the ideal free market. The real debate should be about trade-offs between different objectives, which may be struck at different points in one market or another within any economy, including the communist economies which are now experimenting with free market methods.

The labour market

Labour markets in many countries show persistent disequilibrium. Wages are too high for excess supply of labour to be absorbed by demand. If it were easy to correct such disequilibria, it would already have been done. It is difficult to cut real wages, or lower their rate of increase, because of the impact of nominal wages on prices, because of resistance by labour, and because of reluctance on the part of employers. Freedom of entry into the labour market has been increased by the decline of the closed shop, but the freedom of outsiders to undercut insiders' pay rates operates only to a limited extent. The freedom of the individual employee to operate at maximum efficiency is still in many places circumscribed by employer–union agreements on working practices and production norms.

The public sector plays a crucial part in the labour market in most economies. It is a major employer of labour, and often highly unionized labour at that. Its pay awards have a big influence on bargaining in the private sector, and it cannot so credibly threaten bankruptcy, although it has in most countries increasingly braved resort to dismissals. The public sector also determines much that happens in the labour market by its control over trade union and labour law, covering such matters as bargaining procedures, minimum wage laws and equal pay. The legal privileges of trade unions have been reduced in the UK: minimum pay levels are not so widespread in the UK with the abolition of some wages councils;

statutory pay increases have been lessened in some continental European countries by the deindexation of pay from prices; everywhere in the EC equal pay laws are resulting in relative increases for women which would not have occurred in an unregulated market.

In the private as in the public sector, labour productivity has risen, notably in the UK manufacturing and agricultural industries, but at the expense of employment. Yet the labour market has done a poor job in terms of allocative efficiency as between occupations and regions, because nationwide uniformity within occupational pay structures has persisted alongside traditional differentials between them. Labour is short in South-East England and in excess supply in the North; there is a shortage of maths and science teachers, and a glut of bond traders. Both trade unions and employers' associations impair the free working of the labour market by imposing rigid, monopolistic structures. Kindleberger singles out the German labour leaders as acting with a greater responsibility for the good of the economy as a whole than their counterparts in most other countries (p. 79).

It must be said in favour of the labour market that it shows considerable stability, or at least stickiness, in advanced countries, with pay rates, particularly in nominal terms, varying little from year to year, in the UK for example. In developing countries, on the other hand, pay rates are far more unstable, with high and volatile inflation sometimes cutting savagely into real earnings. Income distribution is as much a function of tax and benefit systems as of labour markets, but tax and benefit systems which seek to achieve a Pareto-optimal post-tax distribution may interfere with other labour market goals. However, it is doubtful whether the cuts in top tax rates in major countries have resulted in much improvement in efficiency. They can be justified by the need for each country to compete for scarce executives — which would not exist if none of them had cut top tax rates below the others — and by the proportional as opposed to progressive concept of tax equity.

The money market

Even the most consistent libertarians jib at complete freedom for money markets. Monetarists in particular tend to see official control of the growth of the quantity of money as a precondition of freedom in all other markets. If monetary control can eliminate inflation, then it can be justified on the grounds that inflation, and uncertainties about future inflation, distort the operation of markets, and the distribution of incomes. Even if, as now seems to be widely accepted, the link between money and inflation is more complex and tenuous than many once thought, there are other prudential grounds for some official control of the money market. Banking systems have some of the characteristics of a public good, providing essential services of money transmission, storage of wealth, and granting of credit, and so it is argued that they should be controlled, and even up to a certain point guaranteed, by the public authorities. The balance between protection of the customer and protection of the bank and its shareholders is a difficult one.

Money markets produce a spurious equilibrium, in which the rate of interest balances the supply of deposits and the demand for credit. It is spurious because of the number of close substitutes for bank deposits and bank credit, of which some, such as the assets and liabilities of building societies in the UK, have been redefined to fall within the definition of broad money. Disintermediation of banks is thus a permanent feature of financial systems, which is intensified whenever monetary controls are attempted. Holders of wealth seek higher rates of return at higher risks than are offered by banks, while borrowers are prepared to pay higher rates of return at higher risks than banks are prepared to accept. Disequilibrium can occur when non-bank financial intermediaries themselves recycle funds into the banks rather than into the hands of non-bank borrowers.

The public sector intervenes in money markets both by regulating banks and by open-market or other operations designed to change the rate of interest. Since the price of money is itself so important for its side effects on other markets, such as those for foreign exchange, housing and capital goods, the authorities change it by working on the supply or demand sides of the money market. They usually avoid short-term volatility of interest rates from hour to hour or from day to day by helping to balance the money market, but by their own actions they may deliberately make interest rates more volatile over a period of weeks or months, in an attempt to stabilize the rest of the economy. They may attempt to offset long-term damage by imposing on the banking system preferential allocations of credit to key sectors of the economy. Such credit allocation may have contributed to the economic growth of the 1960s in countries such as Japan and France, but has now largely been swept aside along with attempts to limit the growth of credit and money in aggregate.

The growth of money and banking markets has meant that 'inside money' created by banks has overshadowed 'outside money' created by central banks in the form of notes and coin, which tends to increase far more slowly. Depositors have a wider range of products and associated services to choose from, at interest rates closer to market rates, with even non-interest bearing current accounts remunerated with free money transmission. Borrowers have a wider choice of loan instruments, even if the structure of lending rates does not fully mirror the degree of risk, partly because of over-rigid official capital adequacy regulations, and partly because of the market bargaining power of large multinational banks and companies.

Stock markets

Stock market prices usually give a short-term equilibrium, in that buyers and sellers of major stocks have to be matched. However, this is often done by the widening of the 'touch' between buying and selling prices, or the 'jobber's turn', which effectively discourages trades by pricing potential buyers and sellers out of using the market. One effect of 'Big Bang' in the London market in October 1986 was to reduce the 'touch' at least in major stocks and shares, thus improving efficiency by reducing transactions costs. The higher volume of transactions, however, contribute on all stock markets to the suddenness of the falls on and around 'Black Monday' in October 1987. The improvement in efficiency was at the cost of higher short-term volatility, although medium-term volatility has always been a characteristic of stock markets.

Freedom of entry into London and other stock markets has been widened by the easing of membership restrictions, and the granting of permission for banks to take over stock exchange members; although in West Germany and Switzerland banks have long been stock exchange members, and in Japan and the USA they still cannot be. Freedom of operation is circumscribed by regulation, which may take the form of supervised self-regulation by professional stock exchange associations. The UK may have set a new pattern by making regulation relatively light in wholesale markets, while seeking to protect the investor — perhaps too much — in retail markets. The public sector can also have a major influence on stock markets by measures designed to widen share ownership, such as privatization issues, or special tax concessions.

The broader issue of the economic efficiency of stock exchanges remains without a conclusive answer. Like other markets, they suffer from information asymmetries of the kind described by Hahn (p. 95). The issuer of a share, and perhaps the agent selling it, know more about the issuing company than the buyer. Since it is impossible for all inside information to be published, it has to be restricted, so that all outsiders have fair and equal access to it. In this ideal vision, the insider is a criminal, whose victim is the outside share buyer missing out on profitable use of inside information. On the other hand, it has been argued that information, like anything else, can be bought and sold (preferably within the bounds of legality), and can and should be used by insiders to drive share prices up to levels which will benefit all shareholders.

There is a parallel dispute about the role of take-overs in a free stock market. Bids are far more frequent in the USA and the UK than in other markets, and this is sometimes taken as a sign of greater good health and vigour. Quite apart from the debatable social side-effects of great (or once great) companies being bought and sold like their own products, there is the argument that shares should be worth the same before as after a bid, because either the existing management is capable of doing as well as its successors or, if not, the existing shareholders are able to change it. The charge against shareholders, and thus the market, is often that they are being short-sighted in selling to a bidder rather than backing the management; this is right only in the sense that a higher bidder may soon come along. The charge against shareholders should be that they themselves have failed to spot the medium-term potential of the company, under either the existing management or a new team; for this the existing management may be partly to blame. The long-standing divorce between shareholders — often concentrated in investment institutions — and managements lies at the heart of at least one type of stock market inefficiency.

Most criticisms of the stock market are addressed to its role as a secondary market in existing stocks and shares. Its efficiency as a primary market for the allocation of new capital funds can also be questioned. In the UK, pre-emption rights for existing shareholders are an onerous restriction on the supply of new money from non-shareholders in the company, for example. Many privatization issues have been greatly underpriced, which has been to the advantage of the underwriters in placing the shares with the public, but to the disadvantage of the taxpayer by short-changing the public purse. Listing requirements, and the attendant expenses, may protect investors, but they restrict entry into the primary market for many small companies. The problem of high risks and information asymmetry in the case of new ventures could be overcome by a revitalization of regional or local stock markets, where personal investors could put risk capital into small companies on which they might acquire first-hand information.

The foreign exchange market

The foreign exchange market, like the money market, has often been seen as the exception to the rule that markets should be free. The Bretton Woods system depended on controls on both quantities and prices, on both foreign exchange transactions and the exchange rates at which they are carried out; the fixed link between gold and the dollar required similar controls on the gold market, with official intervention offsetting those private market movements that were permitted. Since interest rates had to be moved up and down to keep exchange rates stable, monetary controls were subsidiary to exchange rate controls.

When exchange rates were floated in the early 1970s, controls on the quantity of money came into their own as a substitute for the lost exchange rate discipline. Divergent national monetary controls led to ever more volatile exchange rate relationships, except within the EMS exchange rate mechanism. As Lawson says, the behaviour of the foreign exchange market can be destabilizing and disruptive but in recent years the major nations have helped to keep the dollar in line with fundamentals (p. 32). When monetary controls were swamped in many countries by financial deregulation, and the US dollar returned to more normal ranges, exchange rate intervention under the Plaza and Louvre Agreements came back into its own.

The foreign exchange market is one in which speculation on the short-term movement of rates has become a more important driving force than underlying transactions based on trade or capital movements. It is like the money market in that an equilibrium price is always instantaneously reached, but like the stock market in that this price is both volatile in the short term and can become seriously misaligned in the medium term. While the rise in the number of participants has given the market a depth of global dimensions, their tendency to react simultaneously to the same signals has made it more unstable. In developing countries with depreciating currencies, access to foreign exchange, through the black market if not the official market, may drive down the value of the currency still further. Good money drives out bad, and the reverse — Gresham's law — applies only when the exchange rate between the two is fixed at an inappropriate level.

During the heyday of floating rates it was thought that official intervention was powerless to counteract a volume of transactions which might in two days amount to as much as the whole stock of central bank foreign exchange reserves. Even so, short-term smoothing intervention was often carried out, and the EMS provided an example of how successful intervention could be if accompanied by other measures of monetary, fiscal and incomes policies. Lever put a strong case for concerted intervention just before the Plaza Agreement in September 1985 (p. 140). The February 1987 Louvre Agreement has shown that intervention can succeed if it goes in the direction of economic fundamentals — but then what would be the point of it if it were going against them? The central banks have shown how well-commanded smaller forces carrying out surprise attacks can rout a larger rabble of confused and disorganized troops.

Doubts remain, not so much about the effectiveness of intervention, as about the exchange rate objectives which major countries wish to pursue. If all major countries wished to raise their exchange rates to keep inflation down, they might end up with exchange rates little changed, but interest rates higher all round; if this is considered to be a way of curbing inflation, it would be better to agree on a common interest rate policy in the first place, using consumer prices, commodity prices, and other inflation indicators. The USA proposed in October 1987 that a commodity price index should be used as a monetary indicator, and now seems readier to remember what Paul Volcker said a decade age: 'Management of an international system requires that certain rules and decisions be agreed among a number of countries (p. 57).'

Commodity markets

Commodity markets function less efficiently than financial markets, because they have not been globalized to the same extent. For many commodities, domestic prices differ from international prices, and the international market is a marginal and therefore highly volatile one. The response of both supply and demand to price has long and variable time-lags, and this increases the instability of prices themselves. Excess supply is the more common form of disequilibrium, but it can easily switch to excess demand, as in the oil market in 1973–4 and 1979–80. Prices are sometimes driven up by speculative hoarding designed to forestall the expected increases.

Freedom of entry exists in most commodity markets, since suppliers are widely distributed. Oil provides the most successful example of a producers' cartel in recent years, tin the most unsuccessful. The market power which OPEC still has, in spite of the fall in its share of world trade, is bolstered by non-OPEC producers becoming free-riders on OPEC prices — somewhat discounted — yet eroded by non-members' as well as some members' refusal to accept production quotas. For all its fluctuations, the oil market has been more stable than many freer commodity markets, where buffer stock arrangements have repeatedly broken down for lack of financial backing. It is a pity that the main losers from the instability of commodity markets are the developing countries, which can least afford the huge income swings that are caused. The industrial countries have the financial resources, and could develop the techniques, to manage commodity markets at least to the extent that they manage the financial markets, but the political will is lacking.

The EC's Common Agricultural Policy had the political will to begin with, but members were not prepared to provide the finance to manage the market at price levels high enough to satisfy farmers. The CAP has had external diseconomies in that resources have been diverted from more profitable uses, yet its abolition overnight would also have difficult conse-quences for rural communities, which would impose different kinds of costs on society. As the CAP moves gradually towards world price levels, the techniques of market management within the budget are becoming more sophisticated, and political acceptance may be regained — particularly if, as in 1974, EC price levels turn out to be below world market prices at a time of general shortage.

Commodity markets are not good at ensuring either productive or allocative efficiency. Production facilities have to be opened or shut in response to volatile price movements, with higher attendant costs than if a continuous and steady output could be produced. Resources are diverted to commodities which are temporarily in shortage today, and away from those in glut which may be in shortage tomorrow. For example, the high real price of oil in the 1970s encouraged over-investment in nuclear electricity, for which taxpayers, if not consumers, are paying today.

The market economy

The particular markets singled out for attention display both the merits claimed by advocates of the free market, and the defects alleged by its critics. It is often a matter of judgement where the balance should be struck. There are also two separate questions; one is about the direct balance of advantage inherent in the particular market itself, measured by its contribution to employment, GDP, or some other indicator of economic welfare. The other is about its externalities, in other words its costs and benefits to other markets, or to the economy as a whole.

Financial deregulation and the ensuing increase in market activity has brought about sometimes spectacular increases in employment and output in the world's financial centres. Its effects on other sectors of the world's economies are more a matter for debate, as Tobin argues (p. 133). A snap judgement might be that consumers have generally benefited from price competition and product innovation in both savings and loans, while producers of goods and services have had to undergo considerable disruption from unpredictable swings in interest rates and exchange rates as the cost of the price competition and product innovation from which they have also benefited. Since many consumers and producers are at once both depositors and borrowers, a good deal of automatic hedging absorbs part of the shocks, but overexposure in one direction or the other carries higher risks than before.

The move towards the free market has been more gradual and less spectacular in markets for goods and non-financial services than in financial markets. It is easy to underestimate the extent to which markets were already free before the 1980s, and to overestimate the progress of liberalization during the present decade. Privatization in the UK and elsewhere has changed the frontiers of ownership, and given a stimulus to management performance. However, public corporations sell their output in the market just as their private sector successors do, and some of them still have the same degree of market dominance after as before privatization. There are plenty of examples of efficient public corporations, and inefficient private sector companies.

Governments, in the UK and elsewhere, have also retreated from industrial markets by reducing the scope and cost of industrial and regional policies. The cutback in overt subsidies has removed some distortions from the market, although the persistence of tax breaks in some areas has perpetuated others. Governments have stood back from direct intervention in labour markets by renouncing incomes policies, at the same time making them less necessary by changes in the law regulating trade unions so as to diminish their bargaining power. In the UK, the public sector has also been persuaded to make over some of its stock of housing to private owner-occupiers — a generally popular move — but only rather late in the day is the attempt being made to revitalize the private rented sector so that it can make up the shortfall created in the public rented sector.

The free market has in the UK not yet been extended in any major way for non-marketed services such as health and education. The existing minority of private provision is more a competitive spur and a choice for the better-off consumer than a substitute destined to take over from the public sector. This may be inevitable, since the marketing of such services is guaranteed to produce neither productive nor allocative efficiency, may have socially unacceptable consequences, and cannot safely grant the freedom of entry to compete on which other markets are based.

The introduction of market forces is sometimes equated with supply-side economics, and seen as a way of stimulating economic growth. *The Social Limits to Growth*, the title of Hirsch's best-known work,[2] describes some of the defects of this market-driven process, as Oppenheimer points out (p. 21). Many of the scarce resources which Hirsch described as 'positional' goods are either public goods, or can be provided and allocated only by government intervention. Housing in the more salubrious parts of South-East England is a typical positional good, whose value is reduced by being extended to others. The 'not in my back yard' (control) syndrome can be dealt with only by local/government land-use planning, which involves a delicate balance between freedom and regulation. Scitovsky points out that higher spending on positional goods (for example, second-hand houses) does not generate extra employment or income, and is akin to the hoarding of money (p. 156). However, the psychic satisfaction which they give may rise, albeit at a diminishing rate, and thus constitute a welfare benefit to those who enjoy them greater than the cost to those who are denied them.

Income distribution is another positional good of a kind which can be provided only by intelligent government application of the tax and benefit system. The free market is supposed by its advocates to give a Pareto-optimal result, in which changes result in some people being better off, and no one worse off. Hirsch's positional analysis suggests that such comparisons must be made, not just on the basis of today's income against yesterday's, but also by reference to your income against mine. The lowest-income groups in the UK may be better off than they were in real terms, but they are worse off relative to the highest-income groups. It can be argued that, during the 1970s, the highest-income groups became worse off, in relative if not in absolute terms, while the lowest-income groups became better off. The pendulum has swung the other way, but it may have swung too far.

There is a case for adjusting the tax and benefit system so as to give bigger percentage increases lower down the scale in a manner that does not reduce work incentives for the recipients, while having an imperceptible effect on the relative position of the higher-income groups. Sen points out that even highly unequal income distributions may be Pareto-optimal, and uses this to cast doubt on the importance of the Pareto criterion (p. 110). However, economic growth makes it possible to carry out a relative redistribution over time, where stagnation permits only an absolute redistribution, robbing Peter to pay Paul.

The upheavals brought about by the introduction of market forces are not guaranteed to raise the rate of economic growth in the short run. Indeed, as in Britain in 1980–1 and in the Soviet Union today, economic growth may turn negative during a transition period. The UK's growth rate in the mid-1980s gives hope that market forces may be having the desired effect on growth after the transition, in the ways which Lawson lists (pp. 26–36). The costs of growth in terms of unemployment, regional imbalance, and uneven income distribution have so far been judged to be less than the benefits of growth by the majority of British voters at the 1983 and 1987 elections.

Whatever the merits of the market, the British government shows no sign of standing back. The role of government may have changed, but not its importance. Huge tasks lie ahead; the management of the economy and of the financial markets, the regulation or deregulation of the ever-expanding private sector, the provision of a more adequate and sophisticated infrastructure of public goods and services, and the alleviation of the social fall-out from economic progress. The government's task has also been given a new dimension by the EC's programme of measures designed to open up the European internal market by 1992.

Notes

1. Adam Smith, *An Inquiry into The Nature and Causes of the Wealth of Nations*, Glasgow edition, Oxford, 1876, Book IV.ii, p. 456.
2. F. Hirsch, *The Social Limits to Growth*, London, 1977.

Part 1

1 Financial markets and economic well-being: A tribute to Fred Hirsch

Peter M. Oppenheimer

The seven lectures delivered in memory of Fred Hirsch and brought together in this volume span the two broad areas of economic and political inquiry to which most of his professional work belonged: monetary management, both domestic and international; and the relationship between economic mechanisms and human well-being. Fred's friends and those who contributed so generously to the Memorial Fund which enabled the lectures to be commissioned believe a memorial tribute of this kind to be appropriate on account both of what Fred achieved and of what he did not achieve. As a journalist, as an international civil servant and as an academic he stimulated and captivated his colleagues with his insights, his conversation and his sense of humour. He made his mark as an economist and social thinker of international repute. But when he died in January 1978 at the age of 46, he appeared still to be a long way short of fulfilling his potential. From a working journalist living with deadlines he had transformed himself by stages into a professor who (without abandoning his journalistic instincts) devoted five years to producing a major work on economic welfare and growth. Much scope remained for extending and deepening this work and for unifying it with other aspects of economic and social analysis. Fred was very conscious of this. Anyone who knew him personally will recall how in his last two years, when he was increasingly incapacitated by the amyotrophic lateral sclerosis (motor neurone disease) which killed him, he remained passionately anxious to continue working, not as a mere distraction from his progressive disability — though that would have been natural enough — but because he had so much more to say, so many ideas to express about issues of the moment — among them the international economic order, the roots of inflation in a mixed economy and the supervision of multinational banking. The articles he published at that time testify to the range and flexibility of his thinking, even though the loose ends and

Peter Oppenheimer is a student of Christ Church, Oxford, and a University lecturer in economics.

unfinished lines of argument are also conspicuous.

Fred Hirsch was born in Vienna on 6 July 1931 ('shortly after the crash of the Creditanstalt', as he wrote in the blurb to one of his books) and came to Britain in 1934 at the age of three. He was educated at Wilson's Grammar School, London (1941–6), Holloway School, London (1946–8) and the London School of Economics, from which he graduated with a First Class B.Sc. (Econ) in 1952. After a year as a graduate student he moved into financial journalism. From 1953 to 1958 he worked both for the *Banker* (latterly as assistant editor to Wilfred King) and *The Economist*, and then until 1966 full-time for *The Economist*, whose financial editor he became in 1963. His first book, *The Pound Sterling: A Polemic* (1965) attacked the obscurantist attitude to exchange rate policy which then prevailed in British official circles, and indeed in non-official circles, too, where editors of financial journals and bank reviews refused to publish any article advocating devaluation of the pound, because this was regarded as irresponsible and disloyal. In the following year Hirsch wrote *Money International*, a wide-ranging not-quite-textbook on currency and the financial issues of the 1960s. By the time this was published in 1967 (with a slightly revised edition following in 1969), the author had joined the International Monetary Fund in Washington as a Senior Adviser in the Research Department. He remained there until 1972.

At the IMF, Hirsch worked on official studies and reports that were part of the international monetary policies of the day. These included *The Problem of Stabilisation of Prices of Primary Products* (1968) and *The Role of Exchange Rates in the Adjustment of International Payments* (1970, an admirable bureaucratic sequel to *The Pound Sterling*), as well as papers attempting to estimate the need for Special Drawing Rights ahead of the decision in 1969 to make a first allocation of SDRs in 1970–2, and a draft scheme for the consolidation of dollar and sterling balances.

Alongside these heavily political exercises, Hirsch made several contributions to economics, notably an investigation into the determinants of gold production (published in IMF Staff Papers, 1968) and, more important, a joint paper with Ilse Higgins entitled 'An Indicator of Effective Exchange Rates' (*IMF Staff Papers*, 1970). The notion of an effective or 'multilateral' exchange rate measure had been lurking around in economics for a long time. For example, to measure the 1949 devaluation of the pound purely in bilateral terms against the US dollar (from $4.03 to $2.80) and hence to describe it as a 40 per cent devaluation of sterling (the sterling price of a dollar going up approximately from 5s. (25p) to 7s. (35p)) was recognised to be misleading, since many other countries both inside and outside the sterling area, including some of Britain's important industrial competitors, devalued with her. The global or 'effective' reduction in sterling's value was therefore clearly much less than 40 per cent. Closely allied with this point was the distinction, commonplace nowadays, between effective nominal and effective real devaluation, the real devaluation being the nominal one discounted by some appropriate measure of the excess of the devaluing country's inflation rate over the world average. The Hirsch–Higgins paper pioneered the proper articulation of these distinctions, and paved the way for their practical elaboration in the IMF's Multilateral Exchange Rate Model and elsewhere.

In 1972 Hirsch returned to Britain as a Research Fellow of Nuffield College, Oxford. Two years later he became the first holder of the Chair of International Studies at the University of Warwick. As he explained with characteristic humour some nine months before his death in a conversation with Peter Hennessy (the *Times* correspondent and political writer),

I never intended to make the IMF a career because one gets fed up with going to people's leaving parties. Temperamentally I'm not a natural official because of the constraints. In the same way I wasn't a natural journalist because in both kinds of job you have to keep within certain bounds.

Hirsch did not, of course, abandon all his former interests in his new academic pasture. His old firm, *The Economist*, invited him to reflect comprehensively on his experience with the IMF, which he did in a long, signed piece on 'The Politics of World Money' (August 1972). He threw himself into the debate on European monetary integration with essays in the *World Today* and the *Banker* in October–November 1972. He delivered conference papers on the significance of the Eurodollar market for the control of world liquidity (in H.G. Johnson and A.R. Nobay (eds), *Issues in Monetary Economics*, 1974) and on the prospects for an SDR standard to replace the defunct gold/dollar system of Bretton Woods (*Princeton Essay in International Finance*, no. 99, 1973). He wrote (with David Higham) an incisive first assessment of the post-Bretton Woods experience of floating exchange rates ('Floating Rates — Expectations and Experience', *Three Banks Review*, 1974).

His polemics against over-rigidity of exchange rates in the 1960s, and the relish with which he traced the subsequent erosion of these attitudes by the march of events ('The Trial of Managed Money', with Peter Oppenheimer, in Carlo M. Cipolla, ed., *The Fontana Economic History of Europe, The Twentieth Century* Vol. I, 1976) never led him to become a supporter of freely floating rates. Like most economists in the post-Keynesian era, he had until the mid-1970s taken the rationale of monetary and exchange rate management for granted. He was provoked into thinking about it more explicitly by the growing emphasis on financial market autonomy — not merely floating exchange rates, but greater competitive freedom in credit markets — and by the instability and threats of crisis which ensued. His discussion in 'The Bagehot Problem' (*Manchester School*, September 1977) of the relations between competition, supervision and stability in the credit system looks even more appropriate a decade later, when, on top of a world debt crisis, the United States, Britain and to a lesser extent other industrial countries have been caught up in a wave of financial deregulation. These developments, together with the world inflation of the 1970s and technological developments in electronics, have encouraged experimentation and institutional change in financial markets on an unprecedented scale. Doubts have arisen about the ability of central banks and other supervisory authorities to keep abreast of developments and ensure that a proper standard of prudence is maintained by market operators. The essential message of Hirsch's 'Bagehot' paper is that in financial markets some restriction on the degree of competition is optimal. This is first and foremost because of the dynamics of competition in financial markets themselves, and second, because of the relationship between financial markets and the rest of the economy.

Financial markets are characterised by far-reaching asymmetries of information. Banks and other lenders have very incomplete knowledge of the financial soundness of (at least some of) their debtors. Depositors in turn know even less about the risks being incurred by banks to whom they have entrusted funds. As a result, the markets are prone to be affected by herd instinct, rumour and fashion. If the solvency of a major bank or banks appears threatened by large-scale bad debts, the consequence may be a 'run' on other and blameless institutions whose asset portfolios are rumoured to be similarly tainted. As for the linkages between finance and the rest of the economy, history has demonstrated that anxiety about the soundness of the credit system can lead not only to runs on the financial institutions but to a general scramble for liquidity, which means cutbacks in both capital and consumption spending and hence a general reduction in demand for goods and services.

A certain amount can be done to lessen these vulnerabilities by way of deposit insurance on the American pattern, which protects bank depositors while leaving managements and shareholders to carry the risks of unwise lending. But in fact such insurance covers only small and medium depositors; to extend it to large customers is impractical. Moreover, in so far as insurance makes depositors indifferent to the quality of banks' loan portfolios, it incorporates an element of moral hazard like any other kind of insurance, that is to say, it partially renders more probable the contingency against which it provides insurance. The alternative approach to stabilization of the financial system is, as Hirsch's article emphasized, to accept a degree of restraint on competition through some mixture of oligopolistic market structure and central bank guidance or approval, the latter as a *quid pro quo* for protecting banks against runs by means of last-resort lending facilities.

Hirsch's *Manchester School* article constituted, as its title indicated, an updating of Walter Bagehot's century-old insights, in the light of recent work on the economics of information by Kenneth Arrow, George Akerlof and others. At the same time it reflected the extension of the author's thinking and research interests after his move to academe, a development still more apparent in the scope of his other writings. These comprised principally: *Newspaper Money* (with David Gordon; London, 1975); a confidential report commissioned by HM Treasury in 1974 on the breakdown of incomes policy and the pay explosion of 1969–70; *Social Limits to Growth* (London, 1977); and two volumes in which Hirsch featured as contributor and editor, *Alternatives to Monetary Disorder* (with Michael Doyle and Edward L. Morse; New York, 1977) and *The Political Economy of Inflation* (edited jointly with John Goldthorpe and published posthumously in 1978). The feature which unites all these writings is Hirsch's concern with the shortcomings of free markets. His concern was primarily intellectual. He wanted to understand how economic institutions work in practice, and to convey his insights to a wide audience. He had left-wing sympathies. In the conversation with Peter Hennessy cited earlier he explained that his parents had been very active Austrian socialists; and that he himself, having reacted against this viewpoint in his youth, found himself drawn back towards it as he grew older. But he was not a politician. He had no ambition to hold power; and he had no faith in easy-looking remedies. Indeed, he had a rather cynical belief in the tenacity of vested interests, and in the ability of wealthy or otherwise entrenched groups to infiltrate or merely to exploit the operation of public policy in their own interests. Shortcomings of the free market are liable to be matched (and sometimes exceeded) by shortcomings of government.

Such a belief, or insight, is among those used by right-wing apologists to justify a minimalist, laissez-faire approach to government. This reasoning Hirsch regarded as laughably superficial and ahistorical. There is no simple relationship between the scope of government and the harm or injustice that a government perpetrates. Laissez-faire government may be thoroughly oppressive and unjust (as has been demonstrated by more than one country in Latin America), just as socialistic governments like those of Sweden may nurture enterprise while also running a highly developed welfare state.

The relations between freedom, economic achievement and state power were discussed by Hirsch in 'Empty Shelves on the Market Counter' (*Banker*, 1973), a lengthy review of two books by Samuel Brittan: *Capitalism and the Permissive Society* and *Is There an Economic Consensus?* Hirsch took Brittan to task mainly for overstating the capacity of market individualism to maximize unaided the scope of human choice and to fulfil virtually the entire range of human aspirations. A related criticism concerned Brittan's comparative neglect of the distribution of wealth, income and economic power as important issues of social organization.

These questions, albeit debated by Hirsch and Brittan in down-to-earth fashion, are the grand topics of economic and political philosophy. It would have been interesting to rerun the debate after a decade of Thatcherism. This has given the titles of Sam Brittan's books a somewhat *passé* appearance. Mrs Thatcher rejects consensus politics, and she emphatically does not want capitalism associated with the permissive society. Also, in my view, of *passé* appearance is Hirsch's defence of trade union power in British society. Mrs Thatcher's successful curbing of radical trade unionism is almost certainly welcomed by a large majority of British voters (including trade union members themselves). Hirsch would, however, be on strong ground in defending the National Health Service and the public education system against ideological Thatcherite hostility. Both areas are classic domains of 'market failure', where both efficiency and justice require firm limits on the scope of market forces. I suspect that Hirsch would also have scoffed at Brittan's enthusiastic welcome (both as a member of the Peacock Committee on the Future of Broadcasting and elsewhere) for the new broadcasting technologies. Cable and encrypted satellite transmission enable the market to encroach on what has hitherto been a quintessentially public good. Hirsch would not have seen this as an unambiguous step forward in the capacity of the economic system to fulfil human aspirations; he would have wished to consider its impact on the quality of programmes and on the allocation of resources to broadcasting in general.

Hirsch's most challenging and wide-ranging book, *Social Limits of Growth*, is concerned only partly with the shortcomings of competitive capitalism, and it approaches them from a novel standpoint. Hirsch distinguishes between material and what he calls 'positional' goods. This term signifies those goods, access to which depends on one's income relative to other people's and whose supply is, by the same token, largely independent of economic growth and of conventionally measured income levels. Power and status are one type of positional good; holiday villas on unspoilt beaches another. Hirsch argues that, with the increasing satisfaction of biological needs, the relative importance of positional goods increases. Therefore, since the quantity of such goods cannot in general be increased by economic growth (or any other mechanism), the incremental benefits of growth to society diminish; furthermore, the implied frustration of the hopes previously reposed in continued growth reinforce other psychological and institutional defects of the competitive system in undermining its moral foundations (and without putting any worthwhile alternative in their place). What Hirsch has in mind here is first the excessive commercialism of human society, at the expense of relations of trust, friendship and altruism; and second, the growing tension between the pursuit of self-interest which provides the motive power of the competitive system and the moral principles (of honesty, self-restraint, fulfilment of contracts, and so on) which are necessary for the system to remain operable.

Hirsch's arguments reflect intellectual debts to several contemporaries, such as E.J. Mishan, Tibor Scitovsky and R.M. Titmuss; but the emphasis and interrelationships that he develops are very much his own. Would-be critics cannot properly claim that the changes in the social climate observed by Hirsch are the outcome of individual choices freely made. This is because positional goods and other factors such as interpersonal relations involve pervasive externalities, that is, social costs and benefits which diverge from the sum total of costs and benefits confronting individuals in respect of their own decisions. My sense of the worthwhileness of having achieved some positional good typically ignores the accompanying frustration occasioned in (perhaps) a great number of other individuals.

Critics must therefore directly query the distinction between material and positional goods, and/or the proposition that its importance is enhanced by the onward march of economic growth. Whatever specific objections may be brought against them, Hirsch's arguments stand as a bold effort to elucidate the glaring discrepancy between achievement and satisfaction in modern industrial society.[1]

One may conjecture that Fred Hirsch's analytical attention would in recent years have been attracted by two aspects in particular of the world financial scene. First, financial market integration has helped to give the macro-economic policy and performance of the USA a bigger influence on the international economic climate in the 1980s than it has had for the previous 30 years — even though the United States now accounts for a significantly smaller share of the world GNP than it did in the early 1950s. This makes the issue of policy co-ordination, and of the weight given by policy-makers in large countries to international considerations, more acute. The realities of national preferences and democratic politics in sovereign states place narrow limits on what is possible by way of policy co-ordination — which, after all, represents one step (and sometimes two steps) towards supranational government.[2] Hirsch had discussed this and related questions in *Alternatives to Monetary Disorder*, endorsing the view that world economic integration had by now gone way beyond any global political consensus and that, in their struggle to meet national economic objectives, policy-makers were increasingly being tempted to opt out of commitments to a liberal international order. To channel this tendency constructively and prevent it from getting out of hand, Hirsch suggested that it might become appropriate to devise some controlled and deliberate moves to 'dis-integrate' the international economy. The difficulty is to devise a programme which is both feasible and possesses a sufficiently coherent intellectual foundation — for example, to curb what many informed observers consider to be the excessive fluidity and volatility of international money flows, which are an important causal element in the extreme fluctuation of exchange rates and are thereby detracting from the benefits of international trade in goods and services.

Second, the world debt crisis and its management since 1982 have underlined the complexity of the interrelationships between governments and markets in international finance, and the irrelevance of simple formulae such as 'Leave it to the market' or 'No bail-out of the banks'. Whatever the origins of the crisis, the banks, left to themselves, would clearly have precipitated a major financial crash by refusing to renew loans when debtors were in no position to repay. They were held back from doing so by the arm-twisting ('moral suasion') of the principal central banks, led by the Federal Reserve System, in conjunction with the International Monetary Fund and the BIS. This co-operative 'crisis management' was the equivalent of last-resort lending in a domestic banking system.

As it happens, the origins of the crisis lay partly with the authorities and partly with the banks. The authorities initially failed to adapt official channels of international finance to carry a significant share of petro-dollar recycling after 1973. Markets, by contrast, showed sufficient — indeed, more than sufficient — flexibility. Subsequently, the Federal Reserve triggered the debt crisis with the tight money policy imposed from 1979 onwards. This produced a lasting change in the world financial climate which could not reasonably have been foreseen, most notably in raising real international interest rates from a negative figure to around 7 per cent (gross of tax, to be sure, but unfortunately the governments of Brazil and Mexico do not pay American income tax and so could not claim relief). Some 35 countries were obliged to seek rescheduling of their external debts after 1982, in many cases more than once.

The banks on their side made two main errors, both attributable in part to the pressures of competition. First, they allowed the scale and direction of their lending to be determined to an excessive degree by the desire for balance-sheet growth. This meant that they failed to develop adequate criteria for loans to sovereign borrowers, or to perceive the warning light of over-rapid growth in the foreign liabilities of such borrowers (a point since underlined by the theoretical work of Eaton and Gersovitz, Niehans and Sachs, among others). Second, and underpinning the first error, the banks misjudged their ability to lay off the risks of international lending by the use of ingeniously designed financial instruments — as against the traditional procedures of portfolio spread and exposure limits in relation to capital and reserves.

In the 1970s (which means up to 1982) the main instrument was the syndicated roll-over credit, with interest rates adjusted every six months in line with the cost of bank funds (LIBOR). So long as real interest rates remained low (indeed negative) and moved only moderately, the device appeared satisfactory. But with the massive and unexpected rise in real rates after 1979, its main impact was merely to transform interest rate risk into risk of default or outright repudiation. After 1982, the rollover credit gave way to various types of 'securitized' lending, allowing the banks to substitute supposedly marketable paper for earlier non-marketable claims on sovereign borrowers. No doubt the change made the banks feel happier — but the pretensions to marketability of most of this paper would not survive a serious test, because no adequate market is in prospect for it outside banking circles. On the other hand, to the extent that banks have actually withdrawn from longer-term international lending and have been replaced by bond issues on the capital markets, there has been a definite improvement in the nature of credit.

Notes

1. For a sympathetic yet occasionally sceptical review of the work see R.C.O. Matthews, *Economic Journal*, 347, 1977; and the contribution to the present volume by F.H. Hahn, pp. 86–105.
2. While co-ordination can be defined in various ways, it has little substance unless it involves at least one policy-maker adopting measures different in some respect from what would otherwise have been done. For the most part this requires that other policy-makers, too, modify their behaviour, as a *quid pro quo*, so that the whole process yields mutual benefits which are significant and demonstrable. These demanding criteria are fulfilled only seldom and for brief periods.

2 The state of the market
Nigel Lawson

The history of Western civilization cannot be divorced from the development of the market economy. Today, that may sound like a truism. But even ten years ago it would have struck a rather radical note. For over the post-war period, the benefits of the market economy — the benefits of freedom, of choice, and of competition — were increasingly lost from view, in the apparently inexorable advance of the scope and power of the state.

It is not difficult to see why that happened, particularly in this country. The use of state power in the Second World War had led to military victory. Those who shaped post-war Britain saw no reason why the power of the state should not be equally successful in achieving the peacetime goals of economic and social progress. This preoccupation led to the paradox that the post-war economic recovery, which in fact owed much to the unwinding of wartime controls and regulations, was frequently presented as a triumph for planning and control.

The return to the market

The legacy inherited by the government in 1979 was one of 40 years of a fundamentally misconceived approach to economic policy. The post-war consensus was that growth was achieved through expanding the budget deficit, with the state taking a major role in directing resources in the economy, and that inflation should be tackled by direct controls on prices and incomes.

This approach not only failed to deliver economic success. It actually did grave damage to the economy. While inflation rocketed, excessive interference and controls meant that important markets ceased to work properly, and some barely worked at all. That is why the restoration of the market stood alongside the defeat of inflation at the centre of the new

Nigel Lawson became Chancellor of the Exchequer in June 1983. This article is the text of his Institute of Economic Affairs lecture given in London, July 1983.

government's economic strategy when it first took office in 1979, and has done so ever since.

The extension of competition

The most dramatic restoration of the market framework has been achieved through the privatization programme. Already, 17 major businesses, with over 650,000 employees, have been returned to private hands. By the time the privatizations that have already been announced are complete, almost two-thirds of the state commercial sector inherited by the government in 1979 will be back in the private sector. With the unfolding success of privatization, the programme has extended into areas which many people would have thought quite impossible in 1979. Businesses which were once thought natural monopolies, that could be run only by the state, are being subjected, wherever practicable, to competition, and exposed to the disciplines of the private sector.

The extension of competition has indeed been a major theme of the privatization programme, with the licensing of Mercury to compete with British Telecom, the ending of other Telecom monopolies, and now the plan to introduce competition into the generation of electricity. And progress has also been made in breaking down long-established private sector monopolies, such as the solicitors' monopoly over conveyancing and the opticians' monopoly over the supply of spectacles.

An important incidental benefit of privatization has been the boost it has given to wider share ownership. Indeed, since 1979 the number of shareholders has trebled. This in turn should help to improve the working of the equity market by reducing the concentration of share ownership in the hands of a relatively small number of large institutions. The process of wider share ownership needs to go a good deal further. And I expect to see another significant extension as some building societies take advantage of the power to convert themselves into limited companies under legislation enacted in 1986.

In yet other areas of industry, the scope for market forces has been extended simply because the government has deliberately reduced its interference in the affairs of the private sector.

So-called 'industrial policy' under previous governments meant trying to override the market. Governments sought to prop up firms that were dying because there was no longer a market for their product, or because they had been consistently less efficient than their competitors overseas. The argument was, of course, that these firms needed time to turn themselves round. But the practical effect was simply to divert resources from profitable ventures into unprofitable ones.

Traditional regional policies had also proved singularly ineffective in

solving the problems of those regions which suffered from the dis-
appearance of traditional industries. Indeed, they had the perverse effect
of subsidizing capital in areas where the need was for more jobs. And the
counterpart of regional incentives was the bureaucratic control imposed by
the system of industrial development certificates, which throttled new
development in areas where it might have flourished, such as the
Midlands. And various governments' attempts to 'pick winners' bore very
little fruit, wasting taxpayers' money which could have been far better
used by the private sector.

The combined effect of propping up decaying industries and trying to
direct the growth of new ones was effectively to put into abeyance the
market forces which should have been creating and responding to new
opportunities. That is what the government has made room for by
abandoning old-style industrial policy, by abolishing industrial development certificates, and by winding down and recasting regional policy. As
a result, the market is now generating new opportunities and new jobs in
those areas where once it was thought only government could do so. A
wide range of new business is now being set up in, for example, North-
East England and those parts of South Wales which suffered so much from
the decline of traditional heavy industries.

The removal of regulation

Throughout the economy the operation of normal market forces was
constrained in 1979 by a battery of direct controls: controls on prices,
incomes, and dividends, among other things. These were all swept away
at a very early stage. Management was at long last set free to manage;
and the consequent (and long overdue) improvement in the quality of
British management has played a particularly important part in Britain's
economic renaissance.

The most striking example of the effects of deregulation at work is in
the financial sector. The historic decision to abolish all exchange controls
in 1979 opened up a new range of investment opportunities for Britons
wishing to invest abroad, and, by contributing to the improved rate of
return on investment in the UK, encouraged foreign investment in this
country. The abolition of the corset and other controls on the behaviour
of the banks and building societies has greatly increased the flexibility of
the financial markets, and widened the choices available to consumers.
Coupled with that, the changes associated with Big Bang have given the
London markets the freedom they need to maintain and enhance London's
role as the financial centre certainly of Europe, and possibly of the world.

Housing finance, too, has changed dramatically. In 1979, mortgages
were still basically the preserve of a building society cartel, which

maintained a system of mortgage rationing and mortgage queues. This has now been transformed into a highly competitive and innovative marketplace, with immeasurably more choice, and less delay, for the customer. But the new freedom does mean that borrowers have to exercise a great deal more self-discipline about the extent to which they commit themselves than they did previously, and lenders for their part can and should assist in this.

Privatization, again, has massively enlarged the housing market with the sale to council and new town tenants of well over 1 million public sector houses and flats. The remaining challenge is to revive the private rented sector, a classic example of a market suffocated by excessive regulation. The government's proposals to lift restrictions on new tenancies are currently before Parliament. And I decided, in the 1988 budget, to give this long-overdue reform a kick-start by extending Business Expansion Scheme tax relief, for the next five years, to the provision of private rented accommodation under the assured tenancy scheme. I was particularly interested to note today the announcement of the first BES company set up to provide rented accommodation — not in London, but in Glasgow.

The labour market

Perhaps the most serious market malfunction in the years up to 1979 was to be found in the labour market. The proper framework of law which is now in place has transformed industrial relations, and stoppages are at their lowest levels for over half a century. And the continuing rapid rise in the number of people in work suggests that that unhappy phase in our history, when employers saw taking on extra employees simply as taking on extra trouble, is now behind us.

A properly working labour market is the key to more jobs. The superior flexibility of the labour market in the USA is the main reason why American unemployment is so much lower than that of Europe. Although the British market works better than it used to, there is clearly some way to go. A wider spread of profit-related pay, encouraged by the tax relief I introduced in 1987, and better labour mobility following deregulation of the housing market, should both help.

Tax reform

I have mentioned a couple of special tax reliefs which I have introduced, with the aim of helping specific markets to work better. But this approach to tax policy has been the exception rather than the rule. For the starting point in a market economy must be that the tax system should raise the necessary money to pay for public spending with the minimum of distortion to the market economy. That, in turn, means a presumption in favour of low marginal rates and against a proliferation of special tax breaks.

The tax system in 1979 was very far from this idea. Marginal rates, particularly the top rates of income tax, were among the highest in the world — indeed, with the highest rate of investment income standing at 98 per cent, there was precious little scope for any other country's rates to exceed those in the UK. And the 52 per cent rate of corporation tax was made tolerable only by exceptionally generous incentives for investment in plant and machinery, and in certain types of industrial building, which simply served to promote investment driven by tax relief, rather than by genuine commercial considerations.

In 1988, the picture is very different. The UK has one of the lowest rates of corporation tax in the world, at 35 per cent, coupled with allowances much more closely related to the actual depreciation of the asset. As for income tax, the new single higher rate of 40 per cent is among the lowest in the world, and the 25 per cent basic rate is itself the lowest in the UK since 1945. At the same time, a number of significant tax breaks have either been reduced or eliminated altogether.

Progress on reducing the overall tax burden has been rightly subordinated to the overriding need to bring down public borrowing and to maintain a firm fiscal stance. But it is already abundantly clear that the reduction in marginal rates, which is the critical thing for incentives, and the parallel reduction in tax breaks have improved the working of the enterprise economy immeasurably.

Thus, compared to 1979, the UK has a much smaller state sector, less interference in industry, fewer regulations and controls, lower tax rates, and fewer tax-induced distortions — in short, the restoration of the market right across the board.

Of course, much remains to be done: not least, further privatization and still lower tax rates. And there is also the challenge of bringing our free market principles to bear in further liberalizing international trade, through the GATT round, and in shaping the single European market that will come into being in 1992. There are two broad approaches which the EEC could adopt: the bureaucratic one of ensuring that all member states conform to some common system of overregulation; or the free market one of abolishing as many rules and regulations as possible, consistent with a proper legal framework for business. It is vital for the success of the European economy that we go down the second route, and at the same time make our European markets as open as possible to the rest of the world.

For I believe there can be no doubt whatever that the transformation of the UK's economic performance during the 1980s, a transformation which is acknowledged throughout the world, is above all due to the supply-side reforms introduced by the government to allow markets of all kinds to work better.

Markets and macroeconomic policy

So the government's responsibilities in microeconomic policy are clear: to ensure that markets work as well as possible, and then to allow them to do so. Let me now turn to the government's responsibilities in macroeconomic policy, and how these affect the working of markets, and in particular the financial markets.

The Government has to take responsibility for maintaining the value of the currency — that is, avoiding inflation — not least because it is the monopoly supplier of currency. It is an interesting aside, incidentally, that — although all governments *are* monopoly issuers of currency in practice — there is no necessary reason why they should be. In a paper published by the Institute of Economic Affairs some ten years ago, Fritz Hayek proposed, to quote his own title, the *Denationalization of Money*. But this is not a form of privatization that we, or for that matter any other country, have so far espoused, and the government has therefore accepted its responsibilities for the value as well as for the creation of the currency. We have accepted that the state has a clear responsibility to maintain the internal value of the currency – that is to say, to avoid domestic inflation — and, within that context, to maintain the external value of the currency — the exchange rate.

There is nothing new about these dual responsibilities. The heyday of the market economy in the second half of the nineteenth century and the early part of the twentieth was accompanied by a firm financial framework secured by two disciplines. The first was that the state ran a balanced budget. The second was that currencies were linked to gold, which maintained both their internal and their external value.

The first of those disciplines has now, I am glad to say, been fully restored in this country. Its advantages are clear. The balanced budget ensures that the state makes no claim whatever either on the nation's savings, or on flows from overseas. It gives the private sector a stable environment in which to plan ahead, with confidence in the financial stability of the economy — which is, of course, one of the prime objectives of the Medium-Term Financial Strategy. And a sound fiscal policy is an important buttress in maintaining the value of the currency.

As for monetary policy, the ultimate objective — stable prices — is not in doubt. But the means of getting there — how monetary policy should be operated — has proved more complex. Experience in the 1980s has demonstrated that, while the essential thesis — that monetary policy is the only weapon for bearing down on inflation — remains as valid as ever, the practical process of monetary control has been considerably more complicated. The abolition of the various controls within the financial system, which I described earlier, and which has brought enormous benefits, has at the same time made it difficult, if not impossible, to rely solely on monetary targets.

At the same time, the ending of controls inevitably places more weight on short-term interest rates as the essential instrument of monetary policy. For to attempt to reinstate the direct controls of earlier years would not only be needlessly damaging to the financial sector. It would also be wholly ineffective: controls which could even to some extent be circumvented in the 1970s would be all the more easily circumvented in the sophisticated and open markets of today.

Short-term interest rates are of course the market route to the defeat of inflation. At one time it was feared that governments would not be prepared to adjust interest rates sufficiently often, sufficiently promptly, or sufficiently far to enable this process to work. It has been one of the most important achievements of the present government over the years to demonstrate that this is not so, and that interest rates are indeed an effective weapon — both usable and used.

I mentioned earlier that we have to assess monetary conditions as a whole. With separate national currencies in an international financial marketplace, it is inevitable that the exchange rate plays an important part in determining monetary conditions. So governments have to come to terms with the behaviour of the foreign exchange market.

Left entirely to its own devices, we have seen in recent years how destabilising and disruptive that behaviour can sometimes be. The dollar, which of course remains by far the most important international currency, stood at around DM1.80 in February 1980, then rose to nearly DM3.50 at its peak in February 1985, before falling back again to around DM1.80 at the time of the Louvre accord in February 1987. Swings of this magnitude in such a short time cannot possibly be explained by any parallel changes in the fundamentals of the American and West German economies. It is much more that movements in exchange rates tend to be dominated by short-term views.

Yet governments are a part of this particular market, whether they like it or not, not least because they are the monopoly manufacturers of the currencies being traded. And they can afford to take a long view. The experience of the 1960s and the 1970s showed conclusively the folly, and indeed the futility, of governments trying to maintain exchange rates regardless of changes in the economic fundamentals. But what the authorities of the major nations have sought to do with the dollar, with some success, through the Plaza and Louvre accords, has been to help to keep it in line with fundamentals, whether that means a gradual move up or staying the same, and thus to avoid the wild fluctuations which can be so damaging to business and to industry. It is not without interest that — contrary to many expectations voiced at the time, and indeed subsequently, notably after the stock market crash in October 1987 — the dollar is now at roughly the same level against the Deutschmark as it was at the time of the Louvre meeting.

In a free economy, the government has, by definition, very few levers with which to achieve its essential responsibility of ensuring a firm and stable financial framework. And deregulation, with all its advantages for the rest of the economy, has inevitably reduced the number of levers. So it is vital that the available ones are deployed effectively. The government's job, in short, is to deal with the *financial* framework, which it *can* influence, rather than the activities of businesses and individuals within that framework, where any influence it can or does exert is likely to be for the worse. Indeed, I would maintain that, provided the overall fiscal, monetary and exchange rate framework is sound and markets are working effectively, the results of the private sector's economic activity should not normally be something in which it is sensible for the government to interfere.

Current account

If that is so, it has considerable relevance to the topical issue of the current account of the balance of payments. It is clear, first of all, that there are very considerable differences between the present period of current account deficit in the UK, and previous episodes in the UK — or indeed the present experience in the United States. For in the UK now, the government's own finances are very sound indeed. The public sector finances are more or less in balance, even before taking account of the proceeds of privatization. So the current account deficit is clearly not associated with excessive spending and borrowing by government.

No doubt a part of the deficit reflects the fact that the British economy is currently growing a little too fast, above its sustainable rate, and will have to slow down. And as it does, the deficit will diminish.

But that is only a part of the story. For there is no iron law that the private sector's finances must be in balance, in any given year or indeed any given period of years. Sometimes savings will exceed investment; sometimes investment will exceed savings. If domestic savings exceed domestic investment, there will be a capital outflow and a current surplus; if domestic investment exceeds domestic savings, there will be a capital inflow and a current deficit.

Looked at like this, it would in fact be very surprising if the current accounts of the major countries were always in balance. Net capital flows are inevitable and indeed desirable, given that different countries have differing propensities to save and differing investment opportunities. And a country whose investment opportunities are sufficiently attractive to generate a net capital inflow will by definition have a current account deficit.

Some see a current account deficit, nevertheless, as a sign of economic weakness: 'Britain in the red' as the newspaper headlines are wont to put it. But, of course, a current account deficit is manifestly not at all like a company running at a loss. A better analogy is with a profitable company raising funds overseas — either borrowing, or reducing its holdings of overseas assets, or attracting new equity. A company with greater investment opportunities than it could finance from retained profits would look for additional funds from outside. A country in a similar position will draw on the savings of the world, which is particularly easy in today's global markets.

The main reason for the present deficit appears to be that the UK has entered a phase which combines a set of circumstances not seen together for some very considerable time. Investment is rising rapidly. Indeed, the latest survey by the Department of Trade and Industry projects that manufacturing investment will rise by 16 per cent in 1988, as business confidence rides high. Individuals, for their part, have seen their wealth rise sharply in the 1980s. At the beginning of this decade, personal net financial wealth was only about 25 per cent higher than annual personal disposable income, whereas at the end of 1987 it was more than double personal disposable income. It is thus not surprising that individuals now feel they can safely spend more — in many cases by adding to their borrowing rather than by spending their capital. This, too, is in essence a reflection of increased confidence. As a result net saving is low. And consumer spending is running at a high level. This combination of circumstances leads to a current account deficit. But, to repeat, that deficit is entirely the result of private individuals and businesses making choices about their own financial affairs.

And in the same way that the current account deficit has arisen from private sector behaviour, it is likely to reduce through private sector behaviour as well, as the gap between private sector savings and private sector investment closes once more. It is only in the unlikely event of this failing to occur over a sustained period that it would be warranted for the government to intervene by deliberately generating additional public sector savings, through an even larger Budget surplus.

I do not propose to make any forecast about how long this process will take, and how long the current account deficit will last. As everybody who follows the figures will know, it is difficult enough to be confident about what has already happened, let alone what is going to happen in the future! But what matters — and this is the point of using this somewhat extended example in the context of the role of the state in the market — is that, provided the firm financial framework is in place, a period of current account deficit induced by the private sector should give no cause for concern, particularly given the UK's exceptionally high level of net overseas assets.

But the proviso about a firm financial framework is crucial, and has a number of facets. First, it depends on the public finances staying in balance. The current account deficits of the 1970s reflected excessive government borrowing and spending, which it was most certainly the government's job to correct, and which it failed to correct. Second, it means remaining vigilant for signs of inflationary pressures, whatever the source, and standing ready to tighten monetary conditions by raising interest rates whenever such pressures emerge, and doing so to whatever extent is necessary. And third, it implies not accommodating increases in costs by a depreciation of the exchange rate.

Conclusion

The rehabilitation of market forces in the early 1980s was seen at first as an aberration from the post-war consensus, and one that was likely to be short-lived. But I have little doubt that, as a longer perspective develops, history will judge that intervention and planning were the aberration, and that the market economy is the normal, healthy way of life.

Needless to say, belief in the system of free markets does not imply that markets are infallible, any more than examples of irrational market behaviour in any way undermine belief in the market system. What matters is that free markets bring greater benefits, and fewer (and more readily corrected) costs than statism.

And this is a truth increasingly recognized throughout the world: the lesson that the way to economic success is through the marketplace — which means privatization, deregulation, tax reduction, tax reform, and the whole range of other market-orientated policies. Nor is this view confined to governments of the right: it is being vigorously put into practice, for example, by left-of-centre governments in Spain, Australia and New Zealand. Nor indeed is the new awakening confined to the West. China has now embarked on installing the price mechanism, after 30 years of official prices, fixed at the same levels by the State. As the official Chinese newspaper recently put it:

Reasonable prices and rational price structure are formed through market exchanges in line with the requirements of supply and demand law . . . intense market competition and changes in the supply and demand relationship and prices are not bound to the subjective will of government officials.

The Chinese, I suppose, may have had the advantage of seeing the benefits of free markets at close hand in Hong Kong. So the fact that the Soviet Union, too, is embarking in a tentative way on the free market route is, if anything, more remarkable. Mr Gorbachev's recent speech to the special conference of the Community Party of the Soviet Union illustrates how far attitudes are changing:

Regulation by the State was extended to an inordinately wide sphere of public activity. The striving to take detailed centralized planning and control into every nook and cranny of life literally swaddled society and became a serious inhibition of people's initiative . . .
  The slow acceleration of the output of consumer goods can largely be explained by our badly-arranged economic mechanism and by the poor incentives . . .
  A key place in the new thinking is occupied by the concept of free choice.

The whole world is watching with great interest to see what actions follow these words. But the reference to 'free choice' is a significant one. For it reveals the eternal truth that economic freedom and political freedom go hand in hand. Both have been developed in the West, and are now being tentatively extended in the East. And if it is the case that the prospects, not merely for world prosperity but for world peace, too, are better today than they have been for half a century, then historians of the future may well conclude that it was the rediscovery of the power and beneficence of the market which played the critical role in bringing this about.

3 Economic freedom and modern libertarian thinking

Alan Peacock

In introducing thi$ subject, I have been asked to begin by explaining how my thinking on this subject has been influenced by my own experiences as an academic economist, economic consultant, erstwhile civil servant and administrator. If I am to do so, I must say a little about my intellectual background.

My mother was rather nonplussed when in 1941 a high-ranking Polish officer enquired about her 19-year-old son's politics and he was correspondingly surprised by her answer: 'he's a Socialist of course'. At that time, while waiting to be enlisted in the Royal Navy, I was working for a short time at the Colonial Bureau of the Fabian Society and as the unpaid assistant of Dr Rita Hinden, a well known anti-colonialist. As my political interests became tempered by a knowledge of economics, I underwent the familiar transformation of those faced with the competing ends and scarce means problem. However, a student sceptical of received doctrines was an easy prey to Keynesian economics which seemed to offer dramatic, effective and easily understood solutions to the policy problems that concerned me — unemployment and poverty.

As luck would have it, I emigrated southwards to LSE where I was brought face to face with such remarkable figures as James Meade, Lionel Robbins and Frank Paish who had returned from their wartime occupation as economic planners but bringing with them the warning that collectivism was at best an inefficient way of allocating resources . . . Fritz Hayek introduced me to the German 'social market economists' (the so-called 'Ordo-Kreis'), who, wrongly I believe, associated Keynesian economics with all that they had fought against as enemies of the Nazis. Their fear was the corrupting influence of inflation which I believed could be controlled by fiscal policy, but I chose to devote my attention to how to reconcile the liberalization of the economy with my concern for distributional objectives.[1]

Sir Alan Peacock is Professor Emeritus and former Vice-Chancellor of the University of Buckingham. This article is an edited version of the Fulvio Guerrini lecture which he gave in Turin in 1986.

To give economic content to my speculations I wrote a short book on the economics of social security which was rather radical for its day. It aroused the interest of Frank Paish with whom I wrote a number of articles on the economics of social policy: an early attempt to design a workable negative income tax scheme which would replace subsidies in kind; a scheme for breaking the mould of occupational pensions (which appeared, incidentally, in *Lloyds Bank Review* October 1954, over thirty years ago); and a crystal-gazing effort on the economics of an ageing population. Frank taught me how to give proper economic content to my speculations and how to examine their impact on the structure of the economy. I suspect that, like many others, while we appreciated his help and kindness, we owed more to him than we were prepared to admit at the time. He would be much better known today but for his modesty and for the fact that he had a large fund of economic ideas which he gave away as free goods for others to exploit. I suppose that our admiration was qualified by a reluctance to come to terms with his view that a low level of unemployment was incompatible with the control of inflation, though nowadays his 'trade-off' between inflation and unemployment seems to many to have been highly optimistic.

Three things then made me break the mould of my own conventional intellectual posture. It seemed to me that the logical extension of a welfare state based on social transfers was to look forward to the day when the welfare state was not necessary. As I once put it: the proper function of the welfare state is to teach people how to do without it.[2]

Investment in human beings through income support, better educational and health facilities must surely be directed to help individuals to become independent of the state and not to be permanently guided by a patrician bureaucracy. Moreover, even if income transfers were to be needed for a long time ahead, this did not require that school and university education and health services should be government-provided as well as government-financed. In particular, why not finance school education through a voucher scheme, as Jack Wiseman and I jointly proposed in 1964?[3] Why should those able to take advantage of a university education and with a high probability of economic success be given a free investment compared with those who would not have this advantage? Why should parents and university students not be able to choose from a wide range of alternative places of learning at which to study? This was all heresy, except amongst a very few liberal thinkers (mainly congregated at the Institute of Economic Affairs) for whom the word 'competition' was not a dirty word.

The next element in my change in thinking was caused by my experience in government (1973–6) as Chief Economic Adviser in the Department of Trade and Industry. I supposed that free trade and competition policy, a company law which promoted information for consumers and shareholders, and perhaps compensation for firms in difficulties (particularly as a result of some unforeseen change in government policies) formed the essence of industrial policy. I found that senior politicians, both Conservative and Labour, had come to believe in a form of corporatism not unlike that which had developed in Germany under the Nazis or Italy under the Fascists, based on the naive belief that massive government-subsidized investment, primarily in large undertakings, was the clue to economic advance. I soon joined the 'internal opposition' to such policies and had an interesting, exciting but frustrating time trying to erode this view. But I could only fight for my position without my hands tied behind my back if I returned to academic life — which I did.[4]

A final element came from the realization that if I firmly believed in the virtues of consumer sovereignty and its realization through a largely competitive system of delivery of goods and services and, indeed, in economic freedom itself, then I was in a false position if I continued to occupy an academic or government post in which I had complete security of tenure. This was certainly not the only motive for leaving the University of York, where I had been very happy, to become Principal (President) of the only independently financed university institution in the UK — now the University of Buckingham. I had now to practise what I had been preaching. It enlisted my sympathies with all those who start some small enterprise in the hope that it will grow because of the quality of its service, but with all the attendant difficulties of finding capital and of facing a hostile environment created by those in comfortable, established concerns who may use predatory tactics to stifle competition from new entrants.[5]

Today, young economists have full opportunity to be reared on free market economics supplied by first-class minds and do not have to hack through the undergrowth of false ideas for themselves. I do not envy them, for the tests I had to undergo in the form of formidable opposition in academic and public life have perhaps made me more conscious of the meaning and significance of economic freedom than those who have been spoon-fed. I say this with diffidence when I recall that, whatever my own experience, it cannot match that of those who have faced personal danger in the cause of economic freedom.

Defining economic freedom

I have not found it altogether easy to give content to the idea of economic freedom. One way is to begin by considering the economic environment of the individual and what constitutes the process by which he tries to 'better his condition'. Conventionally in economic analysis an individual's satisfaction or utility is a positive function of the goods available to him, both private and public, and a negative function of the effort and skill of acquiring them. His ability to maximize his satisfaction is constrained by the prices of the private goods, the 'price tax' payable for public goods and the prices he commands for his skill and effort. However, such a representation of the individual too easily leads to a model of the economy in which he is regarded as a passive adjuster to his environment — a Pavlovian dog reacting to the stimuli controlled by outside agents. It is gratifying to see the extent to which, under the influence of the Austrian revival,[6] this description of individual behaviour is regarded as both misleading and undesirable.

Economic freedom is first of all a *description* which requires that certain features of the conventional model have particular characteristics. Adam Smith saw this very clearly when he argued, using modern jargon, that the budget constraint on the individual must reflect the domination of particular interest groups. Therefore, the prices of goods and services confronting the individual must reflect competitive forces at work which leave him free to choose alternatives. Likewise, competitive forces in the supply of factor must leave the individual 'free to bring both his industry and capital into competition with those of any other man or order of men'.

The characteristics of competitive markets for both goods and services and factors of production place the individual in the position of being able to loosen the constraints on his actions and focus attention on his activities as a negotiator of bargains rather than as a passive adjuster to forces beyond his control. This difference of emphasis in the conception of economic action is common ground among libertarian thinkers and need not be further discussed at present. Much less certainty attaches to the position of the individual *vis-à-vis* those who supply public goods and those who present him with the bill for them. Before considering modern libertarian positions on this question it is useful to recall the approach to this matter of classical economists such as Hume and Smith. To them the main but not the sole determinant of the size and composition of both public goods and the bill to pay for them was the preservation of the free market itself. If markets were to work in the way which fitted with the description of economic freedom them there must be a well-defined system of property rights, and the costs of contracting between individuals in order to benefit from gains-from-trade would need to be minimized. The promotion of market efficiency was therefore bound to require government intervention. Specialization and gains-from-trade could only take place in a society where the machinery existed for settling disputes and where law and order is preserved, and they were quite clear that in an advanced state of society the principle of division of labour indicated that these preconditions had to be met by government provision of justice and law and order.[7] Smith went further and argued that government had a role in eliminating locational monopolies by the removal of barriers to trade and by 'the expense of carriage' made possible by state-organized financing of road-building and maintenance.

The position of Hume and Smith has frequently echoes in modern libertarian thinking. The emphasis on defining the role of the state not only by reference to its role in promoting 'natural liberty' has its modern counterpart in Nozick's now famous examination of the 'minimal state'.[8] Another example is the condition that as government required coercion, its acceptance required that the rule of law prevailed. The law must be prospective and not retrospective in operation, must be known and certain and applied with equal force to all individuals without exception. Defining the dimensions of coercive action and translating this definition into constitutional rules became the centrepiece of not only the legal but also the economic thinking of the German liberals who formed the *Ordo-Kreis*, to whom I have already referred. It must be noted in passing that German liberal lawyers still defend the view that coercion must extend to destruction of cartels and monopolies[9] whereas American libertarians have argued that anti-monopoly action by the state produces costs of compliance which may be far from outweighed by the benefits of trying to foster competition.[10]

A missing element in the classical discussion appears to be the negotiations connecting the individual with the state, that is to say his part in decisions governing the amount and composition of public goods and methods of financing them. Probably without exception modern libertarian thinkers take it for granted that a description of economic freedom must embody participation in the democratic process. Smith largely ignores this question, but Hume offers the warning that popular governments are more likely than monarchies to create economic conditions which will undermine economic freedom. This arises from the temptation for the state to contract debt without any perceptible fear of bankruptcy because those who have to pay the debts also become the creditors. 'Civilised' monarchies do better. Princes are wary about contracting debt with power-hungry parliaments and it is in the interests of neither to contract debt with foreign financiers.[11] We may not share the classical economists' lack of enthusiasm for popular government, but they do recognize an important dilemma in the association of economic freedom with the political supremacy of individual citizens. If we implicitly accept, as public choice libertarians do,[12] that democratic voting systems are paramount and that the technical problem is how to replicate the competitive market in the choice of publicly-provided goods, no guarantee is offered that the economic system will retain the characteristics that economic freedom requires. The growth of the franchise has allowed the opportunity for the masses to use the public sector as a means for redistributing property rights to their presumed advantage both through a reallocation of fiscal burdens and the transfer of a major part of the capital stock to within the control of government. The paradoxical result has been that the power of government has not increased but decreased. Government is progressively weakened as interest groups within the community are formed to protect their economic interests and form coalitions to buy each other's support for more and more ambitious expenditure programmes which politicians must deliver if they are to retain power. The accompanying increase in the monopoly power of public servants both as suppliers of public goods and factor services to produce them encourages a countervailing growth in collective action by unions and industries as a defence against public monopsony buying. This situation hardly corresponds to a description of an economy in which individual economic freedom is maintained.

Political freedom, therefore, may be a necessary but hardly a sufficient condition for the preservation of economic freedom. Faced with this problem, contemporary libertarian thinking has concentrated on the invention and sometimes the reinvention of constitutional devices to curb the growth of the public sector — 'rules for making rules'[13] In the last analysis, therefore, the descriptions of the dimensions of economic freedom of both classical and contemporary libertarians bear a close resemblance. Their views on the ultimate source of political power may differ; but that power is to be exercised to achieve the same end — to make the economic operations of the state promote economic freedom rather than to undermine it. Why that may be a desirable aim and how it is to be achieved are separate questions which I shall now consider.

The contemporary case for economic freedom

Having outlined the dimensions of economic freedom in contemporary thinking, it seems hardly necessary simply to repeat what are claimed to be its advantages. I should like to concentrate attention more on the differing emphasis on the importance of economic freedom than that which I encountered when I first became an economist.

As I have already pointed out, the support for libertarian thinking among younger economists is much stronger today than it used to be. Typically, my own generation employed welfare economics in order to draw attention to the circumstances in which the government should interfere in the market in order to rectify its 'failures' to deliver full employment, an 'acceptable' distribution of income and wealth and a 'proper' allocation of resources, the last-named being associated particularly with environmental pollution. Few of us were immune from persuasion that there was something of value in the investigation of the dimensions of such failure, and I cannot claim to have been an exception.

Experience in government, which many of my generation have undergone, has made us realize that cures for market failure are often worse than the disease. We are sadder and wiser for not having realized that the types of government intervention commonly advocated rested on totally implausible assumptions. It was believed that those vested with governmental authority would acquire superior knowledge of future economic events and of the intricacies of economic life and that politicians and administrators were endowed with wisdom and integrity which transcended the endowment of ordinary beings. Some still live in hope that, despite encountering government failure, politicians and their advisers might learn from their mistakes. I have already given my own reasons why I believe that there are finite limits to any such improvement and why I was led to reject the economic models which lead us down this path.

The most remarkable change in my lifetime has been the wholesale rejection by a large proportion of younger economists, on analytical grounds, of models of the economy which would support widespread government intervention in order to achieve broadly agreed objectives in Western societies. Their model offers a very different description of the market process which emphasizes the changing preference structures of individuals and the process of adaptation to such change and is no longer based on a given preference structure which implies that one must define the equilibrium conditions inherent in market adaptation. Economic freedom, as I have already defined it, becomes the principal means by which the common measures of welfare record better results than would be achieved if the government sought to control the economy. The remedy for unemployment, for poverty, for satisfactory growth and for consumer satisfaction lies in removing market imperfections, notably in promoting freedom of entry into all factor and product markets. If you wish to have proof of this, let me be a shade parochial and point towards the contents of that stimulating periodical *Economic Affairs* founded by Arthur Seldon. In it the young are in full cry and complain bitterly at the way in which even a Thatcherite government is 'dragging its feet' in its avowed aim to promote economic freedom.

I have no doubt that the young are right in their contention that the market is a superior allocator of resources in the consumer interest, and they would find many Eastern European and possibly Chinese economists who would extol the virtues of the market in this regard. Yet if we were to seek to examine the relationship between the size of the public sector (as an independent variable) and any of the supposed measures of economic well-being, would we always find that the countries with relatively large public sectors perform worse than those in which the public sector is relatively small? Assuming that it is legitimate to employ the usual statistical testing procedures and that there are no problems regarding data collection and cross-country statistical definitions, I would not like to say that conclusive results would be obtained.

I believe that this emphasis on the superiority of economic freedom as a means for achieving collective economic goals is misplaced. For one thing, there is something uncomfortable about the whole idea of expressing libertarian aims in terms of collective economic goals which are traded off against one another and expressed in global percentages such as the rate of economic growth, inflation and unemployment.

For another thing, confining a judgement of economic freedom to its contribution to collective economic goals ignores its contribution to the preservation of liberty and therefore to the creation of those circumstances which, so far as nature allows, give individuals control over their own destiny. As John Stuart Mill wrote in a striking passage:

He who lets the world, or his own portion of it, choose his plan of life for him, has no need of any other faculty than the apelike one of imitation. He who chooses to plan for himself, employs all his faculties. He must use observation to see, reasoning and judgment to foresee, activity to gain materials for decision, discrimination to decide and, when he has decided, firmness and self-control to hold to his deliberate decision . . . It is possible that he might be guided on some good path, and kept out of harm's way, without any of these things. But what will be his comparative worth as a human being? It really is of importance not only what men do, but also what manner of men they are that do it.[14]

It is indeed fortunate that so many of our younger colleagues are able to take liberty for granted and exploit it to the full in their opportunities to develop new ideas and to discuss their policy relevance, facing only the risk that the worst that can happen is that they may be proved wrong. Long may they be able to do so, though perhaps a reminder that 'the price of liberty is eternal vigilance' may be allowed.

Contemporary treatment of common objections

The most common objection to a libertarian position concerns the distribution of property rights. I cannot possibly document the various ways in which a host of writers have attacked the process of free exchange as the ultimate arbiter in the distribution of income and wealth. The focal point of modern discussion is the famous book by Rawls, *A Theory of Justice*, in which, *inter alia*, he states:

The existing distribution of income and wealth . . . is the cumulative effect of prior distribution of natural assets — that is, natural talents and abilities — as these have been developed or left unrealized, and their use favoured or disfavoured over time by social circumstances and such chance contingencies as accident and good fortune. Intuitively, the most obvious injustice of the system of natural liberty is that it permits distributive shares to be improperly influenced by these factors so arbitrary from a moral point of view.[15]

Rawls's own position, in which he advocates the organization of the distribution of property rights so as to conform to the interests of the most disadvantaged group, has itself been the subject of sustained attack by modern libertarians, notably by Nozick.[16] However, the libertarian view does encompass government intervention to alter the distribution of wealth, though its enthusiasts do not sing in unison.

The problem is not one of principle, for the ultimate test of all of us is how far any government intervention represents a restriction of freedom. The problem is one of interpretation. It would be difficult today to find libertarians who would object to some government intervention designed to assure protection of those who are severely deprived. Hayek[17] has argued that so long as 'a uniform minimum income is provided outside the market to all those who, for any reason, are unable to earn in the market an adequate maintenance, this need not lead to a restriction of freedom, or conflict with the Rule of Law'. This still leaves room for much disagreement among libertarians as to the precise level of the minimum and how to decide on who is entitled to receive it. Some supporters of the libertarian position, including the present author, would go much further and argue, along with J.S. Mill, that concentrations of wealth sustained over lengthy time periods can endanger economic freedom, not to speak of political freedom, by the association of such concentrates with the concentration of power of wealthy individuals over the less fortunate.

As I have already indicated, I have devoted a good deal of effort to devising methods by which subventions to individuals can be given in the form of money transfers or vouchers. Individuals then retain responsibility for the purchase of goods and services designed to promote their own welfare and to ease access to education, health and housing. This approach is common currency among libertarians of all generations. I would place equal emphasis on the need to combine this system of economic support with the requirement that those services which are purchased through the transfer or voucher system should be, as far as possible, privatized and freedom of entry should be allowed into their provision so that competition is preserved. Discussion of this requirement is more patchy and I find that German liberal friends, faithful to the nineteenth-century reforms in their university education, are very sceptical about the desirability of privatizing universities and of permitting entry into the university 'business'.

A more severe test of convergence of view among liberals is provided by any attempt to alter the distribution of wealth. One problem is that the issue itself has faded somewhat from libertarian discussion, for two possible reasons. First, growing prosperity in Western democracies and the independence that this affords may make the problem seem less pressing. Second, prominent libertarians, such as Hayek, have discerned positive virtues in the existence of a leisured class with sufficient wealth to promote its detachment from the immediate concern of 'getting and spending' it being 'only natural that the development of the art of living and of the non-materialistic values should have profited most from the activities of those who have no material worries'.[18] We can say 'amen' to that but still, I believe, watch very carefully that the preservation of such a class does not create or re-create some form of hierarchical system — which can happen in communist as well as capitalistic societies — offering particular advantages to the scions of aristocratic families. The problem that I have set myself, and which has never been completely solved, is how to devise public action, for instance, through the fiscal system, which does not result in 'collective redistribution' which takes the form of the transfer of wealth to the state. There is also the familiar problem of what effects any such fiscal action would have on the incentives to work and to save.

I can only refer briefly to the second major criticism of the system of economic freedom, namely that it fails to solve the problem of 'worker alienation'. It may be that the system of economic freedom can countenance attempts by employees alone or in combination to seek to influence the price of their factor inputs and the work/leisure combination, variables which play a crucial part in indiviudal freedom. The fact remains that some form of authority relationship exists between employer and worker in a system which must permit individual ownership of capital and the use of capitalistic methods of production. The hierarchical order at the place of work seems at complete variance with the independence of economic action attributed to the individual by the supporters of economic freedom. Several brief points can be made about this argument:

(a) Libertarians have been quick to point out[19] that the basis of alienation must be technological rather than institutional, for collectivist production, as such a prominent Marxist as Ota Sik[20] has recognized, is certainly not synonymous with the destruction of the hierarchical relationship.

(b) If (a) is true then there may be changes in technology which make possible a change in this relationship. It is interesting to note that in the new technology-based industry there is much more flexibility in work routines and in the extent to which subcontracting may be instituted which promotes self-employment.

(c) 'Two wrongs do not make a right' and if technology does not permit the destruction of the hierarchical relationship in either capitalistic or collectivist production system, then this should not preclude the search for solutions compatible with individual freedom. The point is widely recognized in two lines of thought. The first goes back to John Stuart Mill's famous discourse on 'The Possible Futurity of the Working

Classes' in which he recommended the ownership of firms by the labour force. He set the scene for modern discussion of his proposal by making the proviso that any such system must not destroy competition between firms. The second line of thought is much in the minds of British politicians who, following modern libertarian thinking, wish to encourage the wider distribution of the ownership of capital, not through redistribution, but through the adjustment of factor rewards. Firms will receive favourable tax treatment if they offer payment to workers in the form of profits, adding support to the well-known idea of profit-sharing. Making 'every man his own capitalist' may afford some compensation to those who, in an imperfect world, have to bear the costs of having their work subjected to the close 'policing' which a competitive system may demand.

The taming of Leviathan

The relative growth in the size of the public sector in relation to the private economy is one of the most striking social phenomena of our time.[21] Does it constitute a threat to economic freedom and, if so, what can be done to rid us of this threat? This is one of the great issues directing the debate among libertarians about the appropriate constitutional arrangements to protect freedom as a whole and economic freedom in particular.

I find myself uncertain about the closeness of the correlation between the growth in the relative size of the public sector and the growth in the 'loss of freedom'. Some 20 years ago I gave a lecture on the economics of the welfare state at the University of Virginia. I examined its growth, I pointed to the problems that it created in the formation of strong interest groups and the inevitable bureaucratic inefficiency resulting from centralization of decision-making in health and education. However, I could not bring myself to declare that I foresaw the onset of slavery and oppression in Britain in the name of state socialism. This hesitation clearly puzzled and annoyed those who had invited me.

Subsequently, I think there was a moment in the 1970s when I might have revised my opinion when it looked as if the Labour Party would become the tool of powerful trade unions and of a highly articulate left-wing political group. My present answer to the question that I have set myself is coloured by the fact that there do not appear to be enough self-correcting forces in the economic system to make it certain that the economic interests of taxpayers as voters (and as receivers of state benefits!) will reverse the trend in public sector growth.

This statement is based on an important assumption, namely the present preference structure of voters. Further growth in the size of the public sector is not inevitable but certainly it must depend on a change in that preference structure. From a libertarian point of view, such a change is important and although I may be regarded as too sanguine about the *actual* threats to economic freedom at this moment, to me a relatively large public sector always represents a *potential* threat. It may offer too much of a temptation to those who find power intoxicating and who are clever enough to play off interest groups who look for ways of taming Leviathan.

I mentioned earlier the concentration of effort on the devising of constitutional arrangements to curb the growth in government. I admire enormously the analytical foundations built by such writers as Brennan, Buchanan and Tullock on which constitutional rules for limiting the power of government can be mounted.[22] I would like to think that they are correct in believing that once right-minded people examine their proposals, then efforts will be made to implement them. However, it is difficult to believe that, once such rules are translated into the appropriate downward adjustments in taxation and spending and into changes in the composition of taxing and spending, the 'isolation paradox' will be immediately resolved. All may be generally in favour of limiting the growth in the public sector but they have no incentive as individuals to forgo the benefits of public services which they currently enjoy. It takes great analytical skill to delineate the goals of constitutional reform; it requires a different cast of mind for anyone to attempt the daunting task of describing the path towards these goals and how to find practical ways to induce people to travel along it.

I do not have a complete answer to the problem of linking the goals to the path towards them, and certainly one's faith has to be pinned to a major extent on the hope that voters' preferences will change in the desired direction as a result of libertarian persuasion. I think that a start has been made with programmes of privatizing public utilities and corporations which sell goods and services in the market. However, the important condition attached to such a programme is that there are perceived tangible benefits to members of the public, which are made available in a form in which it would make the public resist any attempt to renationalize the undertakings. I have three broad suggestions about how this may be done. First, privatization must be associated with increasing competition through freedom of entry into the relevant industry. Second, if competitive conditions are difficult to secure, as in cases of 'natural monopolies', then the auction of the property rights must be so conducted that consumer interests are protected, for example by performance bond arrangements and limited periods of franchise operation. Third, the assets of the privatized undertaking must be disposed of to the public but in a way which does not increase the concentration of wealth. Indeed, privatization may offer the opportunity to *reduce* the concentration of wealth by the allocation of shares not to the highest bidder but to the working population at large. It is claimed that this is necessary in the name of the future of capitalism itself and the economic freedom which is associated with it particularly if, as seems quite possible, the relative share of capital as a factor of production were to rise.[23]

Privatization, on sufficient scale and subject to conditions which should appeal to consumers if not to producer interests, is at least a partial means for resolving the dilemma of both reducing the power of the state and of reducing the threat that too great a concentration of wealth might offer to economic freedom.

A concluding note

The concept of economic freedom embraces value judgements about the proper conduct of man — he is responsible for his own destiny — about the objectives of economic activity — the paramountcy of satisfying the preference of individuals. Its supporters are also bound together by the empirical observation that individuals are faced with constantly changing economic conditions engendered by their own evolving preference structures as well as by technological development, neither of which can be foreseen by individuals acting alone or in concert, for instance through collective state action. The combination of the value judgements and the view taken of the workings of the economy produces a notable scepticism concerning both the desirability and the efficacy of government intervention though it presupposes the supremacy of the rule of law.

With all these things in common, the differences between libertarians may be seen in perspective, and appear to be differences in emphasis rather than in substance. But long may we be able to afford the luxury of reasonable argument amongst ourselves and with those who have different views from our own!

Notes

1. For an account of this period in the intellectual history of the London School of Economics and Political Science, see A.T. Peacock 'The LSE and Postwar Economic Policy', *Atlantic Economic Journal*, vol. 10, no. 1, March 1982.
2. See A.T. Peacock, *The Welfare Society*, Unservile State Papers, Liberal Publication Department, 1961.
3. See J. Wiseman and A.T. Peacock, *Education for Democrats*, Hobart Paper no. 25. Institute of Economic Affairs, London, 1965.
4. For an account of my experiences, see A.T. Peacock, *Economic Analysis of Government and Related Themes*, Part IV, Oxford, 1979.
5. See A.T. Peacock, 'Buckingham's Fight for Independence', *Economic Affairs*, vol. 6, no. 3, February–March 1986.

6. A notable example is the work of Israel Kirzner, *Perception, Opportunity and Profit*, Chicago, 1979.
7. See Adam Smith, *The Wealth of Nations*, Glasgow edn, Todd Edition, Oxford, 1976, Book IV.ix.51 and Book VI; and A.T. Peacock, 'The Treatment of the Principles of Public Finance in the Wealth of Nations', in A.S. Skinner and T. Wilson (eds), *'The Wealth of Nations'. Essays on Adam Smith*, Oxford, 1975.
8. See Robert Nozick, *Anarchy, State and Utopia*, Oxford, 1974.
9. T.W. Hutchison, *The Politics and Philosophy of Economics*, Oxford, 1981, Chapter 5.
10. See George J. Stigler, *The Citizen and the State*, Chicago, 1975.
11. See David Hume's celebrated essay on 'Civil Liberty' reprinted in F. Watkins (ed.), *Hume's Theory of Politics*, Edinburgh, 1951.
12. See, for example, J.M. Buchanan, *The Limits of Liberty*, Chicago, 1974.
13. See, W.H. Hutt, 'The Power of Trade Unions' in *The Unfinished Agenda: Essays in Honour of Arthur Seldon*, London, 1986.
14. J.S. Mill, *Essay on Liberty* (1859), Oxford World Classics edition, Oxford, 1942.
15. J. Rawls, *A Theory of Justice*, Oxford, 1972.
16. See Nozick, *Anarchy*, Chapter 7.
17. F.A. Hayek, *Law, Legislation and Liberty*, vol. 3, London, 1979.
18. F.A. Hayek, *The Constitution of Liberty*, London, 1960, p. 130. He endorses this earlier view in *Law, Legislation and Liberty*.
19. For discussion, see C.K. Rowley and A.T. Peacock, *Welfare Economics*, Oxford, 1975, Chapter 4.
20. Ota Sik, 'The Shortcomings of the Soviet Economy as seen in Communist Ideologies', *Government and Opposition*, vol. 9, no. 3, 1974.
21. For a recent exposition of the nature of the growth in government and its causes and consequences, see F. Forte and A.T. Peacock (eds), *Public Expenditure and Government Growth*, Oxford, 1985; and J.A. Lybeck and M. Henrekson (eds), *Explaining the Growth of Government*, Amsterdam, 1988.
22. See in particular J.M. Buchanan and G. Tullock, *The Calculus of Consent*, Ann Arbor, MI, 1962; and J.M. Buchanan and G. Brennan, *The Power to Tax: Analytical Foundations of a Fiscal Constitution*, Cambridge, 1980.
23. I owe this important point to Sam Brittan. See his 'The Politics and Economics of Privatisation', *Political Quarterly*, April–June 1984.

Part 2 The Fred Hirsch Memorial Lectures

4 The political economy of the dollar

Paul Volcker

In view of this occasion, I spent some time in recent weeks reading and rereading Fred Hirsch, and of course came away with a renewed feeling for the strength and breadth of his thinking. Surely few men have so successfully melded command of technical modern economics with insight into the political processes and social setting within which economic policy is framed.

In his last works, Fred battered at the doors of our professional insularities. To carry that work forward will require the effort of more than one man or one lifetime — certainly when that life was cut so short. As one who has practised at the margin of economic analysis and the political processes for some years, I can only appreciate the privilege of initiating this lecture series in his honour.

For a good many years, the world of international monetary affairs was Fred's particular speciality. In an area where much commentary written only a few years ago seems stale and naive, his works continue to stimulate.

Indeed, I was tempted to take as my text today one of Fred Hirsch's last dicta: 'A controlled disintegration in the world economy is a legitimate objective for the 1980s . . .'. The phrase captures what seem to me the prevailing attitudes and practices of most governments in this decade, as they struggle with two central issues that bedevil so much of our negotiations and our actions, not just with respect to money, but over the full range of international economics.

We live in a world in which individuals and businessmen, as never before, have the capacity and the incentive to buy and sell, invest and travel, where they want and when they want — and they want to do so unencumbered by national boundaries. At the same time, modern democracies, at least as much as other forms of government, long for autonomy; they want to control their own destinies in ways responsive to

Paul Volcker was Chairman of the US Federal Reserve Board, 1979–87. These remarks are in the nature of a personal reflection; they do not purport to reflect the official views of the Federal Reserve System or any US administration. This article first appeared in *The Banker*, January 1979. It is an extended version of the lecture given at the University of Warwick on 9 November 1978.

the needs of an electorate often concerned less with national than with local or sectoral interests. Yet, theory and experience indicate that we cannot have it both ways, full integration and full autonomy.

A compromise needs to be struck, and the way we strike that compromise seems to me conditioned and vastly complicated by needed adjustments to another set of circumstances. The United States no longer stands astride the world as a kind of economic colossus as it did in the 1940s, nor, quite obviously, is its currency any longer unchallenged. Now, other centres of strength and power have arisen in the industrialized world, and they will need to share in the leadership. Developing countries have a new economic importance and political consciousness of their own.

A world of more widely dispersed power may have some advantages. But ease of achieving consistent and coherent leadership in the collective international interest is not among them. Intellectually, it is easy to recognize our interdependence. But in practice the instinct is to exert our independence.

Perhaps in the circumstances, the objective of 'controlled disintegration' — modest as it may seem to be — is indeed a legitimate goal. Yet the phrase leaves me uneasy.

I start from the premise that the underlying pressures toward integration and interdependence are growing stronger, not weaker. We cannot reverse or stop the advancing technology that brings us fast and cheap communication and transportation, or the spread of knowledge. Nor can we fail to recognize the sheer gains in economic welfare inherent in a relatively free flow of trade and investment in a world in which endowments of labour, capital, and scarce natural resources vary so widely.

No doubt we can conceive of national economic policies, whether purposeful or accidental, powerful enough to repel the integrating forces. Indeed, in the monetary sphere itself, we seem to have gone some distance in that direction. But let us be aware of the difficulty of controlling disintegration, once fairly started. Already there are temptations to take instability in exchange rates as justification for measure to control or subsidize trade; restraints on trade in turn invite emulation and retaliation. I doubt whether we can proceed very far down that slippery slope while retaining market mechanisms as the main guides to economic adjustments, or without disappointing minimal expectations of rising living standards (particularly among those 'southern' nations only now entering into a 'manufacturing age' which seek our markets). And in time, an increasing sense of commercial rivalry could cloud — or perhaps rather define — political relationships among nations.

The challenge of integration

I do not suggest that we stand on a knife's edge, forced to choose between integration and autarchy. But I would much rather take as my rallying cry, as a focus for necessary negotiations, as an ideal from which to measure progress, the challenge of managing integration rather than disintegration.

I inescapably approach these problems from the context of American experience with the international monetary system, a system in which the dollar has long played a special — in fact an integrating — role. There are those, of course, who would reject the label 'system' as descriptive of the current state of affairs. Certainly, it lacks the sense of agreed structure explicit in the Bretton Woods agreement (a structure, let us not forget, not always paralleled by the actual operation of the 'Bretton Woods system'). Nor does the present system bear much resemblance to the theorizing about floating exchange rates, at least as propagated by the enthusiasts in the 1960s and early 1970s. Indeed, it may not be entirely appropriate to label the system by the single world 'floating', as I shall for convenience, for it has hybrid elements, reflecting in part the absence of a strong consensus on the manner in which it should be managed.

The 'free form' of the present system is hardly surprising, given the circumstances of its birth in early 1973. There was no agreed sense among governments then (and perhaps not even now) that floating provides a basis for a superior monetary system over time, although some officials of some governments had come to hold that view. In the framework of the reform discussions that were taking place before and after the decision to permit the dollar to float, floating exchange rates were eventually relegated to vaguely defined 'special circumstances'.

No doubt the events of early 1973 could be considered one such 'special circumstance' — reflecting an inability to conceive of any other practical way of proceeding at the time. That conclusion was widely shared despite (or perhaps because of) sharp differences about the desired future evolution of the system. But that was not a setting which encouraged governments to give priority to efforts at 'systemization', in the sense of developing agreed codes of conduct within a framework of floating rates.

Support for floating

In the event, floating has of course turned out to be more than a temporary escape valve. Conventional thinking — influenced by the evidence of economic instability all around us — has changed to the point that it finds it difficult to conceive of any general return to officially sanctioned and defended exchange rates. But more than passive acceptance of the status quo is involved. After the end of the reform discussions, successive

American administrations aggressively espoused the floating rate doctrine on its own merits. They had strong support from economists — liberal and conservative alike — within and outside official circles. Mainly schooled in and preoccupied with the economics of a closed (or nearly closed) economy, the economists tended to see floating primarily as a way of freeing macro-policy from the awkward external constraints of the balance of payments. At the same time, they theorized that, in practice, floating rates could provide as much stability as was evident in the latter days of Bretton Woods, or even more. The point had obvious appeal to political leaders with a full plate of domestic problems, particularly if they did not fully appreciate the warnings of those economists who emphasized the importance of price stability at home to the orderly functioning of the system. Some key congressional figures, important because they held a virtual veto power over legislation that would be necessary to implement a new monetary system, became particularly ardent supporters. And important elements of the financial and business community, fearing that the defence of any set of fixed rates would lead to controls on capital or even on trade, provided powerful support. Similar thinking was evident in some other important governments; the allure of autonomy was strong.

The idea of floating as a fully respectable and more or less permanent part of monetary arrangements now has its institutional manifestation in the new Article IV of the IMF Agreement. But that amendment does not provide much in the way of substantive guidance about how the system should operate, beyond rather broad strictures to 'behave thyself'.

There have been attempts, first in the reform discussions and later within the IMF, to specify codes of conduct for the new system, at least in the area of defining rules to govern intervention practices. But these efforts have not gone far enough to have had much influence on actual behaviour. Present arrangements are also, if not quite silent, then reticent on such matters as the size and composition of reserves, the appropriate or inappropriate use of controls, and the like. There is, indeed, acceptance in principle (or perhaps I should say in writing) of the need for international surveillance. But the actual practice, except when countries find it necessary to borrow in the higher credit tranches of the IMF, is undeveloped. In fact, an IMF council of representative national finance ministers, which was intended to provide adequate political authority to the surveillance process, has not even come into formal existence despite years of discussion and authorization in the new articles.

As all reform discussions have made clear, these are matters fraught with technical difficulties. But large as those technical difficulties are, they cannot fully account for the lack of progress in providing a more precise framework for the operation of the present system. Nor can we claim that the operation of the system has been so effective as to render the question irrelevant. Present arrangements have plainly not afforded the sense of stability or speed of adjustment one would instinctively associate with a well-functioning international monetary system. That is as true today, more than five years after its origin, more than three years after the major recession, and at a time when the extraordinary OPEC surpluses have largely been absorbed, as it was in the turbulent 'learning' period.

The need for management

It would surely be wrong to point to international monetary arrangements as the principal source of instability at a time when many national economies have been marked by home-grown inflation, when growth trends have diverged so widely, and when the world economy has had to try to adjust to both the oil shock and the dislocation of the dollar. But it seems to me equally wrong to evade the question as to whether the management — or lack of management — of the system has not to some degree contributed to the instability, or, to put it another way, has failed to provide timely incentives for better economic performance. It does not seem to me an adequate answer to the question to suggest that the system would be more stable if only national economies were stable. Of course, that is true. But, as with chickens and eggs, how does the benign process start?

The contrast between the troublesome performance of present arrangements — at least as measured by the extreme volatility of exchange rates and the slowness of current account adjustment — and rather passive acceptance is striking. It seems to me to reveal much about the problems and preferences of governments in operating a monetary system. Management of an international system requires that certain rules and decisions be agreed among a number of countries, and those participating must have a sense of obligation to conduct their affairs within that framework.

The most sensitive of the rules and decisions involve the exchange rate itself. There is a becoming professional modesty among economists about their ability to approximate equilibrium exchange rates. The views of different countries, looking at the same exchange rates from different perspectives, usually differ. There is no objective way to settle the question. Yet no country today can feel indifferent to the decision. There are direct effects on industrial activity and structure. Support of an exchange rate structure may entail financial costs and impinge upon domestic policy, whether as a result of intervention or because explicit adjustments in monetary or other policies will become necessary. And when financial markets are as open and fluid as in today's world, the potential costs and pressures seem even greater than in the past.

In these circumstances, it is tempting to look to the market itself as an impartial arbiter. If the result is instability, then the potential costs in terms of integration may become relatively high. But balancing the requirements of a stable international system against the desirability of retaining freedom of action for national policy, a number of countries, including the United States, opted for the latter.

Others, particularly smaller countries with open economies, feel differently. Their choices are limited by those of others, and they have a clear interest in binding these larger trading partners to clear codes of conduct. But they have not generally wanted to be bound by rules restricting their own options still further.

The nice question to which I want to return is whether these choices and compromises have, in fact, been appropriately struck — and whether the promise of autonomy, even for the United States, is not more than present arrangements can deliver.

The era of American leadership

The compromise appeared in a vastly different light at Bretton Woods. The world of Bretton Woods was, of course, a lopsided world. The United States emerged from the Second World War with unrivalled economic, financial and political might; across the oceans were devastated and divided nations. Looking back at the disturbed inter-war period, farsighted leaders of both the strong and the weak could appreciate the enormous potential for their own economies in an open, non-discriminatory world paving the way to growth in trade and international investment. A par value system, with exchange rates ordinarily confined in narrow limits, bolstered by international credit facilities and at least the formal obligation for international monitoring and approval of exchange rate changes, seemed the logical monetary component of such a world.

There were, to be sure, strong reservations on the European side to participating so fully in an open world order, given that continent's economic vulnerability. But the economic reservations were overcome by arrangements not an inherent part of the formal structure and symmetry of Bretton Woods, but which plainly recognized the asymmetry of the world as it was. The United States, in effect, held an umbrella over the system. It accepted a long transition period toward convertibility and open markets for weaker countries. A few years after Bretton Woods, exchange rates were fixed at levels that, in purchasing power terms, vastly overvalued the dollar. The Marshall Plan provided the spark and part of the substance for European recovery. And, in the background, the willingness of the United States to assume the major costs of the common defence — and the palpable need for a strong common defence — helped provide the incentive and will for co-operation.

The results turned out to be broadly consistent with the economic and political interests of the United States and its trading partners alike. Leading from a position of strength, the exchange rate relationship was hardly a burden for the United States. Rather, for a long time, it would enjoy the benefits of cheap imports, while its exports (largely of goods that could not yet be produced in volume elsewhere) benefited from increasing buying power abroad. External defence and economic assistance did pose budgetary costs for the United States, but there was no 'transfer' problem. With the international value of the dollar unquestioned, the use of the dollar as a reserve currency provided a ready means for satisfying demand for increased reserves of others without straining those of the United States. It also helped provide the flexibility to meet shifting international economic, defence or political commitments of the United States — and to permit free outward capital flows — without much concern about an external constraint.

Other countries found they could increasingly compete effectively while rapidly rebuilding their economies — export-led growth became the norm for some. While there came to be political qualms, American investment speeded the growth process, helping particularly to bring modern technology and production methods. There was a broad coincidence of political objectives and low defence costs. Most leading countries were able to maintain fixed exchange rates for long periods. The relatively stable level of prices within the United States made the dollar an acceptable unit of value. Both trade and capital flows flourished.

What was not so widely appreciated was that these happy circumstances depended on premises that were not sustainable in the new world the monetary arrangements themselves helped bring about. Viewed in that light, the happy days of Bretton Woods, often viewed today with nostalgia, were a special case, workable because of a particular economic and political setting.

Dollar shortage into dollar crisis

It was symptomatic that hardly were the last books on the 'dollar shortage' published than new authors set to work on the 'dollar crisis'. Triffin, as early as 1959, only a year after the restoration of European currency convertibility, produced the classic description of the ultimate fallacy of operating a system on the basis of increasing use of a convertible reserve currency. The 'Triffin dilemma' inspired a long collective effort to reinforce the system by creation of a new international reserve asset. But as that effort proceeded and before it would be crowned with full success, the persistence of the involuntary payments deficit of the United States raised still more difficult dilemmas in the management of the adjustment process in a fixed rate system, especially when the adjustment directly involved the United States and the dollar itself.

For years, exchange rate adjustment as a means of approaching the dollar problem could barely be mentioned — much less seriously considered — in polite official circles. The instinct was strong, and with justification, that a change initiated by the United States in its own exchange rate was bound to be profoundly disturbing in a system in which the dollar had not only become the leading reserve medium, but a trading vehicle and unit of account for almost all the Western world.

Appreciation of other leading currencies never seemed (to me at least) to provide an answer. It was expecting too much to think then, before inflationary concerns had become so great a consideration in exchange rate policy, that individual countries would voluntarily take the political and economic risks of seeming to write off export jobs and profits so long as they had another alternative. Even as occasional appreciations did appear in the latter days of Bretton Woods, in response to strong market pressures, they inspired a certain ambivalence; the potential small relief to the balance of payments position of the United States from limited and scattered appreciations had to be balanced against the psychological undermining of confidence in the US dollar, risking an unravelling of its fixed position. Actually, of course, devaluations by foreign countries remained more common long after the payments position of the United States came under pressure, persistently working against the efforts of the United States to deal with its adjustment problem.

A natural role for the dollar

The origins of the dollar as a reserve currency antedate Bretton Woods; the design for the post-war monetary system did not contemplate a striking new departure in that respect. Markets, not governmental intentions, make and sustain an international currency; the increasing role flowed quite naturally from the political stability of the United States, its relatively stable economic performance, the sheer size of its economy and its open financial markets. But it is also true that the international use of the dollar was freely accepted by the United States and supported formally by the policy of gold convertibility. As time passed, it came to be seen as a convenient and even essential means for operating a monetary system that was broadly in accord with American economic and political interests.

As might be expected, sensitivity to protecting the stability and international role of the dollar was strongest among the Treasury and Federal Reserve officials directly involved in its management. Their instincts at that time of the first stirrings of the 'gold problem' in the late 1950s were orthodox: concern about the dollar contributed to the relatively tight fiscal

and monetary policies at the end of the 1950s. The recession that ensued
— whatever the reasons for it — helped narrowly elect a new president,
but it probably did not help the cause of orthodox measures to protect the
balance of payments. The analogy of the 'tail wagging the dog' seemed
particularly apt for a continental economy with exports then a little more
than 3 per cent of the GNP.

As it happened, President Kennedy, perhaps partly because he did not
initially enjoy wide confidence in the business community, was himself
instinctively apprehensive of the potential political and international effects
of a dollar crisis (one of his biographers has reported that 'he used to tell
his advisers that the two things which scared him most were nuclear war
and the balance-of-payments deficit'). But there also began to be, for the
first time in the post-war period, a sense of dilemma between 'getting the
country moving again' and maintaining confidence in the dollar.

Impact on domestic policy

For years, the issue could be, and was, dealt with in a manner that did
not seriously compromise domestic policy. The need to protect the dollar
did influence macropolicy, but the influence was felt largely at the
margins (as in the effort to 'twist' short-term interest rates higher in the
early 1960s) or to provide support for major and politically difficult policy
steps that had a plain domestic justification, notably in the fight for a tax
increase in 1968 when concern about the dollar became a clinching argument for a reluctant Congress. From the late 1950s onwards, efforts were
made to reduce the balance of payments effects of the overseas defence
burden and economic assistance. More importantly, against American
instinct and tradition, controls were placed on some capital transactions.

The effectiveness of these approaches was limited in part by the inherent
limitations of such selective measures. But it also seemed to me that, as
time passed, the will to retain or reinforce these measures dwindled as
they more clearly cut into other perceived objectives domestically or internationally. It was symptomatic that, by 1968, the winning presidential
candidate pledged in his campaign to remove the capital controls — a
pledge honoured only after the floating system came into effect — despite
the parlous state of the balance of payments and rumblings of uncertainty
about the dollar. And, as business chafed under the restraints of balance
of payments programmes, so did others within the government who found
room more limited for foreign policy initiatives that had balance of
payment costs. The line was drawn quite clearly at security commitments;
they would not be impaired.

The system held together for a decade and more after the first signs of
weakness, despite the resistance to more fundamental adjustment

measures. International co-operation flowered in the area of new financial mechanisms and improvision to deal with potential points of breakdown — the swaps, Roosa bonds, and multi-country packages of short-term financial assistance to maintain the stability of one currency or another were born during that period. These complex mechanisms had limited economic costs or political risks and could be sustained and expanded over time. Probably more important, but less obvious, was the self-interest of other countries in maintaining a highly competitive external posture, and their perception of the long-term stability of the United States and its currency. American growth and a credible defence posture were important to others than Americans, so there were strong incentives to avoid aggravating pressures on the dollar by refraining from gold conversion — and as the conversions were delayed it soon became evident that conversion on a large scale was no longer practically possible.

Inherent contradictions

But in the end, the inherent contradictions in the system were too great. With the benefit of hindsight, it would seem that an erosion of the competitive position of the United States was implicit in the post-war arrangements. First Europe and later — with even greater momentum — Japan brought its industrial capacity and efficiency close to American standards. It took some 20 years, but eventually the US payments position was irreparably undermined. The full extent of the erosion was never reflected in price indices. But it happened and businessmen and unions knew it was happening. By the end of the 1960s protectionist instincts were aroused, particularly in the labour movement, directly threatening the maintenance of a liberal world order. By that time, it began to look as if no feasible combination of domestic macroeconomic or other more selective policies would offer credible approaches to the underlying adjustment problem, even though cyclically tight money for a time strengthened the dollar.

But the risks of initiating an exchange rate change for the dollar also seemed high, whether viewed from the standpoint of domestic politics or damage to the international system. There were strong doubts about the willingness of other countries to permit a sizeable adjustment, however initiated. So there was no eagerness to precipitate exchange rate action before the need became crystal clear.

Finally, in August 1971, the United States did move decisively to promote the adjustments that seemed necessary. The precise timing was forced by the desire to retain some room for initiative in a situation where the pressures on the dollar were inexorably moving to the point at which inconvertibility would be forced upon the United States in any event. But the way was eased by the fact that decision provided an appropriate setting for a sudden shift in the administration's domestic policies that seemed urgent in its own right, for dealing constructively with protectionist pressures, and for pushing for reforms of trading practices and a realignment of defence burdens.

It turned out to be a contentious period. The historians can debate whether it was unnecessarily contentious: Mr Connally's manner may have grated on some foreign (and a few domestic) ears, but it was no mean feat to manage a devaluation of the proud dollar in a way that did not turn American opinion and policy inward.

The conclusion reached by some that the United States had shrugged off responsibility for the dollar and for leadership in preserving an open world order does seem to me a misinterpretation of the facts. The effort to devalue the dollar externally was accompanied by a programme to deal with inflation internally. The devaluation itself was the strongest argument against protectionism. The operating premise throughout was that a necessary realignment of exchange rates and other measures consistent with more open trade and open capital markets could accomplish the necessary balance of payments adjustment.

The confusion about intentions stemmed in part from the fact that the United States did, for the first time in decades, move to exert strong influence on its own effective exchange rate — something that had not seemed practical under the Bretton Woods system. There was a sense that the United States no longer had the capacity, politically or economically, to accept the position of 'nth' country in the monetary system, passively reconciling the balance of payments objectives of others. Put more concretely, the United States was reluctant to resume convertibility without a reasonable prospect of maintaining a strong enough balance of payments position to support that obligation. That in turn implied the need for a thoroughgoing reform of the monetary system that reflected the new balance of economic power.

Presidents — American presidents — have not in my experience wanted to spend much time on the complexities of international finance. But the repeated charge to the negotiators seemed clear, and in a sense ominous: "I want a system that doesn't have all these crises!' The preoccupation was clear enough: a nation, most of all a great world power, does not want to be hampered in its domestic policies, or in its international security or political objectives, by external economic constraints, and specifically by the need to guard against a breakdown of the monetary system. In other words, the United States wanted an open system, but like others had a taste for autonomy, too.

The Smithsonian pact

To me, the charge to find a crisis-free system could not be satisfied. The passage of time has not altered the judgement. In an open system, the external constraint is there. If ignored for long, a crisis will develop. But a crisis can also be therapeutic — it forces a response.

The first way station in the combined adjustment and reform effort was the Smithsonian Agreement. The problems in reaching that limited agreement provided ample warning of the inherent difficulty of reconciling the varied objectives of different countries when no single participant felt itself strong enough to, in effect, take the risks of underwriting the system.

In retrospect, it still seems a remarkable achievement for the industrialized countries to have agreed together on a new grid of exchange rates. But the agreement was flawed from the start. From an American perspective, the agreement exchange rates (and the barely discernible changes in trade barriers) fell well short of promising the adjustments in the American balance of payments necessary to provide assurance that the new dollar could be maintained, a judgement that seems amply confirmed by subsequent developments. That ended any possibility of others persuading the United States at the time to assume a formal commitment on its part to sustain the new pattern. Convertibility would be left for subsequent negotiations, when its sustainability could be judged in the context of an entire new system.

As a result, neither the economic underpinnings nor the sense of mutual commitment to the Smithsonian arrangements proved strong enough to induce countries to take strong action to repel speculative attack. The British defected by the summer of 1972 with what appeared, by earlier standards in defending a fixed exchange rate, to be relatively little provocation. When an intra-European currency disturbance led to the floating of the Swiss franc and to strong renewed pressures on the dollar in February 1973, the moment was seized to arrange a further general and larger exchange rate realignment — not after months of difficult negotiations as in 1971 but in days.

Attitudes had plainly changed. In retrospect, some of the Smithsonian haggling over minute changes in exchange rates must have seemed ridiculous; the earlier changes had neither helped nor hurt as much as had been anticipated. To me at least, the new exchange rate pattern this time did seem economically appropriate and defensible. But by that time there had been too many changes in exchange rates too frequently to make any fixed rate easily credible. It had become evident, in the midst of the crisis, that official inhibitions on floating were fast diminishing. When the United States devalued, both Japan and Italy found it easier to respond by floating than by taking the political responsibility of fixing a new exchange rate.

There was already a strong strand of opinion within the American administration sympathetic to floating, and that opinion began to find some echoes elsewhere. As inflation gained momentum, some surplus countries, in particular, saw their efforts to restrain their money supply undercut by the defence of a fixed rate. Moreover, there was no urge to settle unresolved disputes about the form and nature of convertibility obligations in a new monetary system in the heat of crisis. So, when the new rates came under attack in the market, the alternative of permitting the dollar to float for an indefinite period no longer seemed so unthinkable a step. The industrial countries were tired of trying to make a fixed exchange rate system work, at least without reaching fundamental agreement about the manner in which such a system would work.

Spreading the burden of adjustment

The American proposals that provided most of the focus for the ongoing reform negotiations were designed to develop the logic of a par-value convertibility system suited to a more symmetrical world. Part of the American preoccupation — and that of others — was to develop even-handed pressures on surplus and deficit countries for adjustment. Others were preoccupied with ensuring that the United States, as the most powerful country and the provider of the reserve currency, could not evade discipline. These concerns on both sides for a fair sharing of responsibilities seemed to require more continuous, stronger and more explicit international surveillance than that to which Americans or others had been accustomed. And even with significant new elements of exchange rate flexibility, there was an implication of the need for closer co-operation of demand management, and particularly monetary policies.

The particular role of the dollar in a future system was a source of confusion in the discussion. To some, providing a reserve currency had aspects of what General de Gaulle had long before termed an 'exorbitant privilege', and, more technically, they were fearful that it could delay the need for American adjustment. The United States looked at the other side of the coin; other countries could refuse adjustment by piling up dollars and thrust the Americans back in the 'nth' country position. In the last analysis, most other countries did not seem to want to give up all the flexibility in reserve management afforded by reserve currencies, nor did the United States want to lose all the element of elasticity provided by some use of the dollar. So, at times, it seemed possible that the basic positions were not so far apart. But the negotiators never fully resolved the more technical questions of how outstanding dollars would be consolidated — a matter of direct and visible financial consequences for participating countries — and the larger question was dropped with the reform effort.

Why agreement could not be reached

The vision of a highly structured new monetary system that emerged from that debate may rest on the library shelf, but three observations drawn from that debate and subsequent events still seem relevant. First, in the last analysis, the practical politician, already struggling with intractable domestic problems and pressures and looking toward a murky future, does not want to be bound by more rules and obligations than absolutely necessary — and the more precise and complicated the rules, the more difficult to reach agreement. Large and small countries alike resisted the requirements for heavy and explicit surveillance from without and for policy co-ordination — all under the oversight of a rather anonymous supranational body, that, in the eyes of domestic legislators, would lack political weight or even legitimacy. In concept, the need for these disciplines could be recognized. In practice, the way the rules would be defined was crucially important to all, but views about just which rules were important did not easily coincide.

My second observation is that the reluctance to develop a highly structured system does not mean the underlying issues will not return. Indeed, I believe they are returning, for they are inherent in the management of any international monetary system.

Third, the difficulties of writing a rule book for a highly structured system, combined with simple observation of the divergences of policy and performance in the real world, suggested that floating could be — indeed would have to be — more than a safety valve. If imperfect, it need not be the disaster that so many looking back at the 1930s feared.

By and large, that has been the way it has worked out. From the standpoint of integration, growth in trade has slowed, but not necessarily more than could be explained by the slower growth in worldwide GNP. Amid all the turbulence in exchange markets, financial markets have successfully recycled massive amounts of funds from OPEC and other surplus areas to points of need in the developing world and elsewhere. The general trend of exchange rates has been broadly in the direction of changes in purchasing power parities — in other words, real changes in exchange rates have been generally smaller than the nominal. And the real exchange rate changes have themselves generally been in a direction suggested by structural or cyclical payments imbalances.

Quite obviously, the industrial world has had more inflation and less growth over recent years than that to which it had grown accustomed. But those problems clearly had their roots in earlier developments, and it seems to me a fruitless exercise to try to compare what has happened with what might have happened under some quite different system.

But I do think we can say, with some confidence, that, whatever the net balance of pros and cons, experience had begun to reveal some potential difficulties more reminiscent of the flavour of the 1930s than of much of the theorizing.

Pulling back from floating

For one thing, we have learned that even large exchange rate changes have not been nearly as effective as hoped in achieving adjustment of long-standing imbalances in current account positions. Where clear improvements have been made, they can be traced mainly to changes in relative demand pressures, or to structural changes such as North Sea oil. I do not doubt that trade and current account positions will in time shift in response to real exchange rate changes, but I believe we are learning that the process takes a number of years — possibly even a decade — to work its way fully through the economic structure.

At the same time, there is little evidence that floating exchange rates have substantially dampened the tendency for changes in business activity in one country to affect the trade of others. Changes in income continue to dominate current account balances in the short run. The shifts in current account positions may exert a pronounced influence on exchange rates, but the exchange rate movements will not, in turn, have much impact on cyclical imbalances. Indeed, for extended periods, J-curve effects may be perverse.

Above all, we have seen again and again what some had forgotten — in these circumstances exchange rates can be dominated by expectations of what they will be tomorrow, or next month, or next year. And, those expectations will be volatile when divergencies in national policies seem pronounced, or when those policies are subject to great uncertainty. If in these circumstances markets come to believe exchange rate stability is not itself a significant policy objective, we should not be surprised that snowballing cumulative movements can develop that appear widely out of keeping with current balance of payment prospects or domestic price movements.

At that point, free floating exchange rates, instead of delivering on the promise of more autonomy for domestic monetary or other policies, can greatly complicate domestic economic management. Strongly depreciating currencies will reflect but also exaggerate inflationary forces; in an inflationary world, appreciations may assist efforts to stabilize the domestic price level, but they will undercut efforts to deal with the other side of the 'stagflation' dilemma. As uncertainty infects domestic as well as international financial markets, business decisions to invest slow down.

But it is not only domestic economic management that is affected when swings in exchange rates lose touch with underlying price and interest rates relationships. When patterns of trade or capital become influenced by monetary fluctuations rather than lasting comparative advantage, the underlying rationale of a liberal trade and investment order is undercut. The point is not merely theoretical. The instinctive political reaction in the face of seemingly capricious impacts on one industry or another is to protect or subsidize domestic industry, or to impede the flow of capital.

Major nations have wisely and repeatedly pledged themselves during this disturbed period to maintain open markets. By and large, they have resisted the pressures to turn inward. But we cannot be blind to the evidence that, under strong pressure from monetary instability as from other forces, the fabric of discipline is fraying at the edges.

I do not depart from the strong consensus that we have, on a world-wide scale, no other practical choice than to work ahead within the broad framework of a floating system — and that system offers the most promising framework for 'managing integration' as far ahead as we can now see. It seems to me particularly suited to a world in which the major adjustments, in trading patterns and in political thinking and organization, required by the dispersion of economic and political power have not yet been completed.

Money will not manage itself

But, at the same time, we have had plain enough warning of the fact that international money, any more than domestic, will not manage itself. It will deliver neither the promised autonomy nor integration if we fail to deal with some of those issues that were unresolved in earlier efforts at more structured reform.

In quite different ways, the monetary initiatives under way in both Europe and the United States reflect a new appreciation of the dangers. A European Monetary System and the forceful programme to stabilize the dollar at home and abroad can help point to solutions. I would like to suggest, in a very general way, how we might build on those initiatives in several areas.

The exchange rate is the most visible and sensitive manifestation of an international monetary system — and exchange rates inherently involve the interests of more than one country. A floating rate offers two enormous advantages in a world of uncertainty, and where more than one sovereignty is involved; it requires neither explicit international agreement nor a closely defined commitment to defend. For larger countries, these advantages are likely to remain decisive. But they do not negate the fact that, at some point, left to themselves the swings in market rates can become so large as to damage the growth and stability of countries with both depreciating and appreciating currencies.

We cannot identify with any conviction or agree upon an 'equilibrium rate'. But it should be possible over time to reach a broad consensus about levels of a few key exchange rates that are *not* acceptable — that are plainly disruptive of mutual objectives. I refrain entirely from the semantics of target or reference rates, which imply more confidence about identifying a central tendency or a narrower range of fluctuation than is warranted today, and a formality of obligation that is beyond our reach.

Framing a proposal

What I have in mind is more in the nature of quiet mutual contingency planning. Clearer understanding of a few leading nations among themselves about what extremes of fluctuation are mutually tolerable, and which should be strongly resisted, would seem to me to enhance the prospect for effective domestic policy-making, as well as lay a base for more stability in international markets. After all, we have the example before us of even the largest country, the United States, finding that it had to care when it found its domestic policy undercut by extreme exchange rate movements — a lesson long ago learned in the United Kingdom. At the same time, a sense that extreme fluctuations will be resisted and reversed could help stabilize market expectations, and thus reduce the risk of those extreme fluctuations developing in the first place.

I do not suggest that merely stating the objective will produce the result, or that there should be any public commitment to particular rates. It will be action that counts. In that connection, intervention alone seems to me a relatively weak reed upon which to lean; it will be effective over time only if more fundamental policies support the objective. Prolonged and massive intervention itself, of course, has implications for domestic monetary policies. But, in the end, if we are serious, domestic policy measures will need to be brought more consciously into action. The lesson of experience is that those instruments will, sooner or later, need to be used with force when markets become disruptive. At that point, the risks to the domestic economy may be greater than if more marginal changes were made earlier, before market uncertainty becomes so great and expectations perverse.

In an American political context, it has been a difficult matter to bring these considerations of exchange market stability to bear on a Congress or even an executive preoccupied with the domestic economy. In retrospect, the case can be made that, more often than not, a more forceful response to pressures on the dollar would have ultimately been helpful in promoting domestic, as well as international, stability. Experience in late 1972 and early 1973 — when policy was slow to recognize the impending inflation-ary explosion — is one case in point. A floating system, unlike a convert-ibility system, does not flash its warning signals in a way that more or less demands a prompt policy response, but we need to learn that the warning is there none the less.

There seem to me implications for the way we organize ourselves for economic policy decisions. I alluded to the tendency in the United States to think of domestic and international economic policy as distinct, and the latter as the tail on the dog. The analogy is less apt as time passes, and the economy of the United States has become so much more exposed to external developments. Yet, partly by the accident of personalities, partly by explicit organization, the responsibilities for, and direct exposure to, the international side of the equation have sometimes been lodged with those most influential in domestic policies and sometimes not. Historically, the main preoccupation of presidents themselves in the international arena has understandably been with security and political matters; the international dimensions of economic policy have not had the priority many foreign leaders attach to them. The situation is further complicated by the dispersion of responsibilities in the committee system in the Congress, where there are no mechanisms for looking at international economic policy as a whole, or for regularly blending oversight and legislative responsibility with those for domestic policy.

Institutional insularity

No doubt comparable problems exist in other large governments. But my experience strongly suggests that our mix of policies will be more effective as those responsible for the external side are also in the mainstream of domestic policy-making.

Obviously, the characteristics of economies differ in their exposure to foreign trade. A looseness of exchange rate relationships tolerable for some countries with relatively small external sectors may not be so desirable for others which feel more exposed. One approach toward reconciling those different needs is inherent in the current effort toward a European Monetary System. Clearly, that effort has more than economic dimensions — it is part of the larger European ideal and a matter for European decision.

As Fred Hirsch emphasized some years ago, the transition towards a European system could pose difficult problems. I hope we will all be alert to dealing with the complications that transitional period could present for international co-operation on a wider scale, to protecting the legitimate role of the IMF, and to the implications of decisions within Europe for the monetary systems as a whole. But I see no inherent conflict with the needs of the international system once the new regional system is fully effective. One important group of countries will have achieved conditions of monetary stability for the greater part of their trade. In economic relations with the rest of the world, Europe would be in much the same position as the United States and Japan with respect to trade and external influence. In those circumstances, with Europe speaking with one voice, a harmonious approach toward the international system could be easier than before.

There does seem to me a latent danger — no part of the intention of present European leaders — implicit in the development. Regional monetary unity implies a greater degree of visible loss of autonomy for member countries; yet national economic problems will remain. The temptation could arise to solve some of these regional adjustment problems within Europe by direct subsidies to producers, by protection against the outside world, or by other means damaging to the trading opportunities of others.

In the last analysis, the United States, Europe, and Japan have similar endowments of skills, technology and industrial plant — their comparative advantages *vis-à-vis* each other are not immense. (Ironically, where they are greatest, in agriculture, some of the largest barriers to trade exist.) At the same time, they are each heavily interdependent with the Third World. In theory, a process of disintegration within the *industrial* world could probably go a long way without intolerable damage to their economic welfare. But it is hard to visualize that process without it also leading to intense national competition for the markets and materials of developing countries. It would not be a pretty picture.

The dollar overhang in perspective

In considering the sources of the recent monetary disturbances, I recognize the point has been made that the very large proportion of dollars in official and non-official balances held for international purposes is partly a vestige of the old system, and a desire to diversify can potentially become an independent influence on the stability of current arrangements. However, the forces that motivate decisions to diversify by a foreign dollar holder are, in the last analysis, no different from those bearing on the decisions of those holding the vastly larger stock of dollars in the United States. And, experience suggests that, as the dollar strengthens, concern about diversification dwindles.

For those reasons, emphasis on the 'dollar overhang' as a special problem has often seemed to me misplaced, for it could easily divert attention from the need for more fundamental measures to maintain confidence in the dollar generally. The vigorous domestic and international measures in support of the dollar recently announced by the United States, including some sales of US government obligations denominated in foreign currencies abroad, can relieve pressures from the direction of diversification, as from elsewhere.

If the problem is indeed more structural, it does not seem to me one for American concern or action alone; if so, the preferred option for the United States would in all likelihood be the opportunity to earn back any excess dollars through a current surplus. There is something unedifying, moreover, about some central banks taking full advantage of the flexibility afforded by present arrangements to place their funds where and when they choose, while complaining at the same time about instability in the system.

In a floating system some of the particular concerns in a convertibility system about controlling the volume and composition of international reserves appear in a different light and may reasonably have lower priority. But that should not mean that, with the collective instruments at hand, progress could not be made under international auspices toward achieving an appropriate balance between the supply of dollars and its desired use in official reserves.

Who will manage the system

All of this raises questions of governance — if the system is to be managed, who will do it and how. The obvious institutional focus is the IMF, and it plainly has a full plate of work ahead. I have long felt that if that work was to proceed with full effectiveness, the effort of the international bureaucracy — however able, and it is very able — needs to be reinforced by more active regular participation by politically responsible officials of member governments. That is, of course, the rationale of the council authorized by the new articles. To a degree, the function has been performed on an interim basis by the advisory council. But it would seem to me useful, more than symbolically, for that body to assume now full legitimacy by transforming itself formally into the council and renewing the sense of commitment to develop its surveillance function.

As a practical matter, that body will be too cumbersome and too far removed to deal adequately with some of the continuing issues of exchange rate and economic policy management that arise among the leading industrial countries, nor could it really hope to have the kind of political authority in those countries necessary to make the process work most effectively. That gap can be filled, it seems to me, only by more or less continuous consultation among the 'trilateral' countries: Japan, Europe and the United States. And the consultation must extend to the highest level. The recent practice of 'economic summitry' points that way.

The value over time will not, I suspect, lie primarily in particular decisions reached at particular times; in fact, one of the potential problems with summitry is that when world leaders meet together on a special occasion there is an artificial pressure to respond to public expectations by dramatic new initiatives, even when the most sensible and realizable objectives may be more modest. Instead, the most important result can be in the less public process of exposure to each other's problems and viewpoints, working against the natural bias to focus primarily on the internal consequences of economic policy.

This may seem a modest programme. All of it grows directly out of the logic of recent practices, market developments, and governmental decisions. But if commitments to the approach were meaningful — if those recent initiatives are interpreted not just as isolated events but as frank recognition of the fact that the recurring issues of monetary stability cannot be shrugged away — then I feel confident that, in the end, the floating system will come much closer to the ideal of reconciling of our domestic and international objectives.

This turbulent period started with two dollar devaluations. I thought then, and think now, that they were necessary to lay the base for needed adjustments in the world economy. But they also, perhaps inevitably, helped upset expectations and loosen disciplines. We have not yet been able to restore a firm sense of stability.

Today, a stronger and stable dollar is plainly in the interest of the United States and the world. These recent months have, if nothing else, been instructive to all — a sliding dollar undercutting our own anti-inflationary effort, generating uncertainty at home and abroad, hurting growth. There has been a sense of drift, of a lack of control or direction in the monetary system, infecting and reinforcing other sources of economic instability.

Now we can see the beginnings of a new base. It cannot rest on the actions of the United States alone — for it is no longer the dominant power of Bretton Woods. But its strength can be joined with others to provide fresh impetus and a renewed sense of commitment to a stable international order. An objective of 'managing integration' may thereby not sound so Utopian after all.

5 Responsibility in economic life

Charles P. Kindleberger

The aspect of responsibility I propose we think about is the extent to which, under our mixed capitalist-government intervention systems, the individual person, household, or firm is responsible for the system beyond the duty of conforming to explicit rules. Do we, that is, have an economic responsibility for the public as well as for our personal private welfare? I propose to discuss the issue first at the level of a national economy of households, firms and government, and then to apply the analysis to the world.

Let me begin with Adam Smith and his 'obvious and simple system of natural liberty'. Once this has been established:

Every man, as long as he does not violate the laws of justice, is left free to pursue his own interest in his own way . . . The sovereign is completely discharged from a duty . . . of superintending the industry of private people, and of directing it towards the employments most suitable to the interests of the society.

Dr Smith himself, of course, had reservations. In discussing corporations, he observed that private interests were too strong to allow the restoration of freedom of trade in Great Britain, stating that to expect it was as absurd as to expect an 'Oceana or Utopia should ever be established in it'. He had some harsh words for the 'mean rapacity, the monopolizing spirit or merchants and manufacturers, who neither are, nor ought to be the rulers of mankind'; and for the 'sneaking arts of underling tradesmen' who employ chiefly their own customers, as opposed to 'a great trader' who purchases goods only where they are cheapest and best. Implicit in these and similar passages is the admission that 'natural liberty' may at least on occasion lead the economy astray.

Two hundred years after *The Wealth of Nations* we still cling fairly generally to Smith's conclusions about the beneficent outcome of the market, although the analysis has been qualified and broadened in various

Charles Kindleberger is Ford International Professor of Economics Emeritus at the Massachusetts Institute of Technology. The article is a shortened version of the Fred Hirsch Memorial Lecture given at Warwick University on 6 March 1980. It first appeared in *Lloyds Bank Review*, no. 138, October 1980.

ways. The theory of public goods implicit in his 'certain public works and certain public institutions which it can never be for the interest of any individual or small number of individuals to erect', has been extended from magistracy or law and order, national defence, and roads and bridges to income distribution, where the market may yield a result unsatisfactory from the viewpoint of welfare, and to stabilization, where the fallacy of composition, of which more presently, means that individual households and firms, maximizing their private interest, may harm the general good. Moreover, between the private goods of individuals and firms, and the public goods produced by the sovereign as an act of duty, there is room for collective goods, sought by aggregations of individuals or firms to advance the welfare of the particular group.

Smith's insight that it would not pay individuals or small groups of individuals to erect and maintain certain works or institutions has been generalized into the 'free-rider', who lacks adequate incentive to contribute or work for the production of public goods. Private and collective goods are produced because their benefits outweigh their costs to the producers; public goods are forthcoming because the sovereign fulfils his duty. In democracies, political scientists warn us, they may well be under-produced because of the free-rider. Public goods are available for all to enjoy whether they bear an appropriate share of the transactions costs necessary to their production or not. The individual or form maximizing its own welfare will hold back from carrying its share of the cost, unless it is forced to do so through the police powers of the state. If there are enough free-riders, the bus never gets out of the garage.

The fallacy of composition

The fallacy of composition was first borne in on me in the first edition of Samuelson's *Economics, An Introductory Analysis* (New York, 1948), and in particular his treatment of the paradox of thrift. Thrift is good for the individual and the household — at least in a period of stable prices. But when everyone tries to save more, the economy may save less as it goes into recession and incomes fall. The problem is more general. Individuals pursuing their private and collective interests may interfere with one another. This is especially the case for collective goods, where an increase in monopoly profit reduces consumers' surplus and total consumption, and in free-riding, where the individual, conserving his energy for his own purposes, inhibits the production of necessary public goods.

The Chicago school of sociological economics is using economic reason-ing to illuminate a number of problems that were formerly dealt with by sociology or political science, for example, education, procreation, crime, voting in democracies. Rational, maximizing behaviour in this approach views, say, the law in a detached fashion. One obeys the law if the mean of the probability distribution of being caught times the likely penalty of being convicted is greater than the benefit from ignoring the law. Or one departs from a short-run profitable action with untoward public consequences only if it should happen that the feedback of those consequences in the long run is negative, and has a present discounted value, at some appropriate rate of interest, that is greater than the short run profit that must be forgone. Government is provided by politicians who can earn higher returns in this fashion than by work in private industry, or by 'leaders' who maximize a different argument in their objective function than income or wealth, perhaps *gloire*, immortality, lust for power, and similar non-economic drives.

I find the Chicago school altogether unpersuasive. As a counter-example to the theorem that profit maximization is all, let me suggest voting. Voting has positive transaction costs: one must take time and go to the polls. Moreover, the benefit of voting for the individual is derisory. Virtually no issues of consequence are decided by one vote. Accordingly, the costs to the single person outweigh the benefits and no rational person will take the trouble to vote. It is true that many people do not vote, and some nations, such as Australia, make voting compulsory in order to overcome the free-rider. At times and places, votes will be bought as part of a collective good. For the most part, however, and within limits, people vote, and do so as a duty, as part of their political responsibility. What is more, while there are venal politicians in democracies, and in monarchies as well, many persons present themselves for elective office as a chance to serve the public.

My thesis is that economic, like political responsibility, take two forms, one passive, obeying the law and acting in ways that can be generalized, to uphold the categorical imperative of Immanuel Kant and defeat the fallacy of composition; and one active in the form of positive leadership. Both are present in varying degrees and at various times in national economies and the world economy. An adequate supply of both is necessary if the economy is going to function well.

Before I pursue the argument, I wish to place on record an admission of a strong prejudice in favour of market solutions to the greatest feasible extent. When it is working effectively, the market is a beautiful device for the decentralization of decision-making. Moreover, the analysis that underlies the defence of the market is highly useful as a pregnant hypothesis, to use Karl Popper's expression, serving to illuminate many problems in which behaviour can be analysed as if (*als ob*) man responded in a rational way to income-maximizing motives. The presumption in favour of freedom for markets from regulation or intervention is perhaps weak; it is merely that the burden rests on people who oppose it to prove that they have a superior device for allocating factors of production to activities and the resultant outputs to end uses. The arguments in favour of the market are not conclusive, but experience shows that, like marriage, honesty, democracy, old age and a few other tried and true institutions, while far from perfect, the market is better than the available alternatives.

Passive responsibility

While self-interest within a framework of government regulation provides a useful first approximation to a description of the economic system, and even a working hypothesis for the solution of many economic problems, more is needed, and in particular a certain amount of self-restraint in some areas, voluntary compliance when enforcement cannot take us all the way in others, and active economic responsibility on behalf of the system as well.

Let me take the problem of income tax. I am no tax expert, but it is clear that income tax in the United States, to the extent that it works well, relies on voluntary compliance. The Internal Revenue Service (IRS) is completely inadequate to police the millions of tax returns, even with the help of social security numbers and computers. Enforcement through audit or prosecution takes place from time to time, but on a scale so limited that there is strong incentive, at least for certain types of income, to fail to report in on cost–benefit grounds, the benefit of the tax saving being greater than the present discounted value of the chance of being caught times the penalty. There are indications that the tax system is breaking down in the United States, with a large black market in labour and goods, not to mention a white market in barter that seems to exist outside profit-and-loss statements in which income subject to taxation can be calculated. IRS lawyers work continuously to close old loopholes, while collective interests lobby to protect the old and create new.

The fallacy of composition plus the need for equitable and consistent application of rules pose another problem. Most rules need exceptions for the hard cases. The difficulty is that the existence of loopholes for exceptional cases sooner or later attracts the attention of the run-of-the-mill participant for whom the rules were devised, who then claims the loophole for himself on the ground of non-discrimination. Numbered anonymous Swiss bank accounts served a laudable public purpose when they were illegally maintained by German Jews, fearful of expropriation. They are a threat to society when the system expands to accommodate criminals and other tax evaders. A small outlet for emigration is desirable in enabling citizens of a country thoroughly out of tune with the values of their society, and possibly persecuted for their behaviour, to leave. But to generalize emigration or immigration — to make it available to anyone —

threatens to overwhelm or even destroy a state, as the creation of the Berlin Wall in 1961 and the illegal inflow of Mexicans into the United States today demonstrate. Murray Weidenbaum has written in praise of tax havens, and there may be justification for them within highly restricted limits. Generalized, however, they destroy the state and the capacity to produce public goods, and enthrone individual self-interest together with economic irresponsibility.

The fallacy of composition for collective interests can be illustrated with organized business or organized labour. The latter had its origin in defence against the former, but, as so often happens in multi-person games, two antagonists ultimately team up and war against a third. The individual litterbug can claim to have no impact on the beauty of the landscape except as the first beer can in a location attracts others, and the single taxpayer who fails to report income in cash hardly affects the budget balance of a given year, but large trade unions can more readily be accused of achieving private gains at the expense of the public goods of price stability and sustained employment. Virtually every labour leader would deny that any union or combination of unions has responsibility for the economy as a whole. That is the task of government, they insist, even when their power frequently prevents the government from restraining unions. Or if the rise in the price of oil means that real national income must be reduced (in the United States), each union is likely to insist, along with all other organized groups in the society, that it is justified in seeking to ensure that none of the reduction falls on its own members.

Indexation, maintenance of wage differentials, exceptions to wage guidelines in collective bargains are the order of the day. In progressive industries, unions ask for the whole increase in productivity, while in lagging industries wages have to increase at the pace of the average to prevent loss of the work-force. With no one willing to accept wages below the average increase in productivity, the average drifts upwards. There is the view that, after the war, German labour leaders were responsible men who exercised great restraint in their wage demands in the short term to stimulate expansion, stability and greater rewards in the longer term. The alternative view, however, is that these union leaders were not so much responsible as their unions, after a decade or more of Hitler and war, were weak.

Or contemplate Sheik Yamani, the Saudi representative to the Organization of Petroleum Exporting Countries, who appears on a number of occasions in the last decade to have been trying to hold down the price of oil in the interests of world macroeconomic stability, as opposed to maximizing short-run returns. Again there is an alternative view that reality differs from appearances, and that Yamani is a master of public relations fully committed to raising prices as fast as anyone else. It is none the less possible that a monopoly may set a price lower than that at which marginal cost equals marginal revenue as it worries about possible feed-backs, perhaps only that of encouragement to new entry, but conceivably that of world recession with its consequences on the long-run demand for oil.

Acting responsibly for unions or firms, however, has the disability implicit in the prisoner's dilemma. If unions hold wages, corporations may not behave in such magnanimous fashion but raise prices and profits anyhow, to make the short-run sacrifice of labour nugatory. Or, as Saudi Arabia expands oil production to make up for some of the shortfall from turbulence in Iran, Kuwait among the low absorbers may cut its produc-tion further to thwart the attempt to hold down prices. Economic respons-ibility on the part of one actor may merely encourage greater short-run maximization of another, without achieving the public (and long-run private) purpose sought.

This is nowhere more strikingly illustrated than in the lender-of-last resort role that Hirsch illuminated in his striking paper on 'The Bagehot Problem' in the *Manchester School*, September 1977. The issue is called 'moral hazard' in the field of insurance. When an individual firm or household is fully insured, it has less incentive to be careful. Banks confi-dent that they will be rescued if they get into trouble are less wary about staying out of it. The mean of the probability distribution of disaster may rise but the penalty arising from disaster is reduced. There are devices to correct for moral hazard-deductible limits and required self-insurance in the fields of fire and casualty. In life insurance, the policy holder presumably has a big stake in the outcome, just as the pilot and crew have in the safe operation of aeroplanes — a fact from which I have often taken comfort. The insistence of government, central bank or an organization like the Federal Deposit Insurance Corporation in the United States that it will save only sound banks and lend only on sound collateral is not persuasive. First, it is analytically awkward, confusing a general-equilibrium problem with a partial-equilibrium one; in a financial crisis with falling prices, soundness is a function of how fast the lender of last resort responds. The longer it waits, the further prices fall, and the less sound are banks and their collateral. Second, however, as the crisis deepens it is necessary to rescue the sinners with the faithful, since their fates are linked.

One answer to these game-theoretic problems is to have rules, spelled out with great clarity, as to how banks should invest their funds, and how insured policyholders should protect their property. In collective bargain-ing, the proposal is for a social contract under which each sector of society, and each segment of each sector exercises great self-restraint in return for the promise of others to act similarly. As in any cartel, the problem is enforcement, how to prevent marginal units from chiselling or, as I prefer to view it, competing.

Swedish and Dutch experience with social contracts goes further than that of most countries, but has been marked by wage drift, profit drift, and, in the case of the Netherlands, wage explosion after a lengthy period of constraint. In addition, there are serious problems of finding the appropriate initial conditions that represent a sort of stable equilibrium because they embody wage differentials agreeable to all. Most unions are likely to assert that once their prospective negotiations are completed with a hefty raise, providing all other collective arrangements are unchanged, and provided prices stabilize at the present level, they will be pleased to accede. But the fallacy of composition assures us that there is no time when all will agree that now is the exactly right time to enter into the social contract. Correcting lags of some wages behind others, in an attempt to get the differentials right, illustrates the problem at its clearest.

The question of size

Thus far we have been discussing economic responsibility in terms of the fallacy of composition, with the implication that if a party is small and operates with no feedbacks or external effects with no fear of creating a precedent, and is unlikely to give rise to demand for equal treatment on the grounds of consistency, it may be tolerable to permit free-riders or exceptions to general rules on the ground that no significant consequences would follow. This may be open to criticism on the ground that it allows the ends to justify the means and, that in law and in morality, small is big because precedents are set and consistency is needed. One cannot let small unions as in municipal transit get away with standard-breaking wage increases, because if any one group gets huge rents, all will insist on having them, too. But there are two aspects of the question, related to what has just been said and to each other. What if the actors are large and conspicuous?

Large is almost definitely equal to conspicuous, but not quite. It depends on the setting. Young people will behave differently in a big city than they do in their home village because they are anonymous in the former and known in the latter. In New York, there is likely to be no feedback from loud and raucous conduct, provided one stays clear of the police, whereas if one were to behave in the same way in Belmont or Lincoln, Massachusetts, the fact would be noticed, commented on, remembered. Observation affects behaviour — the Heisenberg principle allied to social science — in other ways. Some football players do better in the game on Saturday than they do in practice during the week, unobserved. And some firms behave more circumspectly when they loom large in a small town than when they fade into the background in the metropolis, or their actions may differ as between when they are, and are not, required to disclose their operations. It was long said of one major American corporation — I think General Electric, but that may be simply bad memory — that it was unwilling to have the only major factory in a small town because that inhibited its behaviour too drastically, as the community came to depend on it unduly. General Motors' response to the brouhaha raised in the early 1950s over its profits from the ownership of General Motors-Holden Ltd in Australia was to buy up the remaining minority stock and convert from a public to a private company which did not have to publish accounts — until that escape was cut off by Australian legislation requiring private companies owned by foreign corporations to publish regular reports.

Size and conspicuousness are two dimensions affecting economic responsibility. Age and status are others. It is useful to distinguish between old money and new money, between the Establishment and the upstarts, between — at the level of individuals — the aristocracy or gentry and the *nouveaux riches*. Age, the Establishment and *noblesse* all *obligent*, that is have responsibilities that extend beyond those of the average citizen or firm. In the money dimension, of course, age and *noblesse* are highly correlated, apart perhaps from southern Europe where impecunious aristocrats are looking for heirs or heiresses to marry. The path to the gentry lay through business or financial success. But with gentlehood or aristocratic position went obligations along with perquisites. There is a certain amount of hypocrisy about this, and it is easy to be cynical about the Christmas baskets handed out by the lady of the manor which failed to deal effectively with any real social problem. None the less, it seems to be useful to observe the greater responsibility of the successful than of the unsuccessful, and of the old successes as compared with the new.

This leads us to a form of economic sociology diametrically opposed to sociological economics. The magistracy required to make the system work comes from the value system, not from maximizing behaviour. Passive conformity to the spirit of the rules is part of responsibility; readiness to take a role in enforcement and in adapting the rules to new circumstances is another and more active part of it.

Active responsibility

How does economic responsibility come into being? In my judgement it responds more to Keynes's law that demand creates its own supply than to Say's law that supply creates its own demand. My emphasis on size, prominence, position in society, the reactions of others, and so on, suggests that it is pressure that pushes government into new functions, and peer pressure that pushes non-governmental bodies into positions and attitudes of responsibility. It is of great interest to me that, in the last century and prior to the foundation of the Federal Reserve Act, the leading

New York money market banks behaved differently than other banks in New York such as the trust companies and savings institutions, and than out-of-town banks of all descriptions. The larger group depended on the money-market leaders to provide them with cash in crisis, and the leaders knew what they were supposed to do, and prepared to meet the responsibility.

The conclusion is more general. More basic an incentive than maximizing income and wealth is obtaining the approval of one's peers. As David Riesman has suggested, most actors in today's society are outer-directed, conforming to the standards set sociologically in productive as well as consumption behaviour, and those that are inner-directed are merely running on the outer-directions received at an earlier stage and internalized. This last thought explains the responsibility of *noblesse oblige* and the responsibility of old money, although it must be admitted that some who might have been guided by tradition turn out to be more susceptible to the blandishments of the jet set in the outer-directed mode.

There is a problem here, however. To develop economic responsibility one must choose the right peer group. There is, after all, honour among thieves, and one sociologist of my acquaintance explains much anti-responsible behaviour in France on the basis of the 'delinquent peer groups' that grew up in that society in defence against strict parents and strict schools. People are drawn into academic life, business, the professions, government, and crime by choosing different models to ape, rather than each maximizing income and wealth — as the Chicago school would have it — in different ways. The point is neatly illustrated by the behaviour of two firms in the same industry toward high-level employees on their release from jail after serving sentences for criminal conspiracy against the anti-trust acts. Though the employees of the two firms had been convicted of conspiring together, one firm, seeking the approval of its employees for loyalty, gave their men a rousing welcome, new jobs and made them heroes. The other company, interested in being judged against a different standard, fired its group.

Economic responsibility at the national level, in this reasoning, is maximizing income and wealth within the constraints of avoiding behaviour which cannot be generalized, complying with the spirit as well as the letter of the law, watching feedbacks through the rest of society, and example-setting. Such responsibility is generated by success, but old success that has settled down and internalized class authority and pride. It is difficult to achieve in young economies, or aged ones, the former because responsible standards have not yet taken sufficient shape, the latter because there are too many groups struggling for collective goods and the fallacy of composition overwhelms them. Despite Adam Smith and the Chicago school, profit-maximizing economies with too few dedicated leaders with insufficient individual commitment to voluntary compliance, and collective groups prepared to restrain their demands will not function. This seems to me the insight of Fred Hirsch in his book with John Goldthorpe on the *The Political Economy of Inflation* (London, 1978).

I have not left much time for economic responsibility on the international front, but this is hardly necessary as I have written a number of times of 'leadership' in the world economy. In its active form, responsibility is leadership. François Perroux has written of dominance in international trade and investment, referring to the United States. Political scientists refer to the leadership role as 'hegemony'. On the left wing the expression is exploitation and neo-imperialism. In my judgement, Britain in the nineteenth century and the United States from perhaps the Tripartite Stabilization Agreement in September 1936 to the two-tier system in 1968 or the Connally *shocku* of August 1971 acted responsibly. It was in their interest to do so because of feedbacks and a low rate of interest on future trouble. There is a debatable question whether both countries benefited enormously from the position or paid something of a price in losing freedom of action, higher taxes for defence, carrying the free-riders who held back paying a proportionate share of the world public goods of economic stability and peace.

The elements of economic leadership at the world level have been spelled out: an open market for distress goods, and a stockpile of accessible goods that are in short supply, in crisis only, not as a regular device for stabilizing prices; a counter-cyclical or at a minimum stable flow of capital (and aid) to maintain the flow of international purchasing power to all parts of the globe; management of exchange rates and of macroeconomic policies through the gold standard operation by the Bank of England in the nineteenth century, and the dollar standard of Bretton Woods after 1947: and finally the lender-of-last resort function, as illuminated by Fred Hirsch in 'The Bagehot Problem', preventing deflation from spreading through the system by holding upright a critical domino — be it bank or money market — at the right time. It was these requirements of responsibility that Britain could no longer discharge in the inter-war period, and that the United States then hung back from, that made the 1929 depression such a traumatic episode in world economic history.

I have not resolved in my own mind whether economic responsibility can be widely shared. Certainly at the moment when the United States' capacity for leadership is diminishing and West Germany and Japan are fully responsible in the passive sense, but unwilling to take a forward role, one cannot require small countries or the newly rich to undertake very much of the costs of maintaining the system. We are blessed by having few boatrockers of the Bismarck-Hitler-Stalin-Hirohito — even de Gaulle — stripe who would produce a drastic change in how the system operates. Iran, the PLO, Qadaffi, the New International Economic Order are not powerful enough to rock the system beyond the capacities of OECD countries to restore it to balance, provided that consensus on policy emerge rapidly rather than a stalemate. But such a position as in the International Monetary Fund where the United States, the European Economic Community and the Group of 24 each has a veto suggests that active economic responsibility may be a scarce good in the years ahead.

Economic responsibility goes with military strength and an undue share in the costs of peacekeeping. Free-riders are perhaps more noticeable in this area than in the economy, where a number of rules in trade, capital movements, payments and the like have been evolved and accepted as legitimate. Free-ridership means that disproportionate costs must be borne by responsible nations, which must on occasion take care of the international or system interest at some expense in falling short of immediate goals. This is a departure from the hard-nosed school of international relations in political science, represented especially by Hans Morgenthau and Henry Kissinger, who believe that national interest and the balance of power constitute a stable system. Leadership, moreover, has overtones of the white man's burden, father knows best, the patronizing attitude of the lady of the manor with her Christmas baskets. The requirement, moreover, is for active, and not merely passive responsibility of the German–Japanese variety. With free-riders, and the virtually certain emergency of thrusting newcomers, passivity is a recipe for disarray. The danger for world stability is the weakness of the dollar, the loss of dedication of the United States to the international system's interest, and the absence of candidates to fill the resultant vacuum.

I beg you to excuse me from discussing Britain's responsibility to the European Community, and the price that is being charged you for it. That is your problem, and I do not envy you it. I hope, none the less, that I have interested you in the concept of economic responsibility as an essential ingredient of economic life, along with income and wealth maximization, and a legal framework in which every man, firm, bureaucrat and nation can pursue his, her or its interest.

6 Reflections on the invisible hand

Frank Hahn

Introduction

That a society of greedy and selfseeking people constrained only by the criminal law of property and contract should be capable of an orderly and coherent disposition of its economic resources is very surprising. Marx called such a society anarchic and so it is. Yet, ever since Adam Smith, economists have been concerned to show that such anarchy is consistent with order and indeed with certain desirable outcomes. Smith proposed that the market system acted like a guiding — an invisible — hand. It was invisible since, in fact, there was no actual hand on the rudder. The metaphor which he chose was exactly apposite.

Two hundred years on, the basic theory has been much refined and we know a good deal more about those instances where the hand trembles or fails. Yet there is no agreement on some of the fundamental ingredients of the story and there is also much which we simply do not understand. In this lecture, I shall give my evaluation of our present theoretical state in this matter and draw a number of lessons of a somewhat practical kind.

Although I shall be concerned with theory, the practical significance of the subject is self-evident. It certainly is at the centre of a great ideological divide. It matters a good deal whether Mrs Thatcher or Mr Benn, or for that matter President Reagan, are appealing to coherent and grammatical arguments when they espouse the market or the planned economy. Certainly non-economic considerations, for instance, the fate of liberty under either system, are involved. But even these cannot be evaluated and argued about until we can describe and understand the economic stage on which the scenarios develop. In any case, it would be a pity if, for instance, we embarked on large and portentous changes in our society on the basis of arguments as flawed and incomplete as those recently presented by six of Mr Benn's supporters. It is also undesirable that we should allow Mrs Thatcher to engineer large reductions in employment

Frank Hahn is Professor of Economics at Cambridge University. This article was delivered as the Fred Hirsch Memorial Lecture, given at Warwick University on 5 November 1981. It first appeared in *Lloyds Bank Review*, no. 144, April 1982.

and national income on the basis of an unsubstantiated belief that this is required for the invisible hand to do its job. All these people take it for granted that somewhere there is a theory, that is, a body of logically connected propositions based on postulates not wildly at variance with what is the case, which support their policies. It must be of some significance to enquire whether this is in fact so.

To do this, I shall have to give some account of the pure theory of the invisible hand as formulated now. I shall need this as a benchmark but I shall keep it short since its main outline is probably familiar. I shall then take up what seem to be important objections to this theory or significant lacunae. I shall lastly try to support the view that, on our present state of knowledge, it would be prudent not to place all our eggs into one or the other of the ideological baskets on offer. To some, this conclusion will appear wishy-washy and unpalatable; I shall want to argue that it is reasonable.

The pure theory of the invisible hand

We think of a society where private property and contracts are adequately supported by law. The economic environment of any one person is fully specified once the prices of all tradable objects are given. These prices give the terms at which one good can be exchanged for another and it is a basic assumption that all individuals can trade to any extent they wish at these prices. One notices that the economic information is conveyed very economically — the individual knows everything that he needs to know once he knows prices.

However, for the pure theory which I am now considering one has to make the unpalatable assumption that there are terms of exchange given for every pair of goods which an individual might wish to exchange. In the textbooks this assumption is formulated to read: markets are complete. It is a very important postulate and Keynes, for instance, placed great emphasis on the fact that he did not invoke it.

To understand the significance of the postulate of complete markets, one has to understand the economic classification of goods. It is obvious that butter today in Warwick is, from any trader's point of view, not interchangeable one for one for butter today in Cambridge. So, certainly, we want to distinguish goods not only by their physical characteristics but also by their location. But butter today in Warwick is not, from any trader's point of view, the same as butter tomorrow in Warwick. So we must also distinguish goods by the date at which they are available. However, we are not yet through. Butter today in Warwick when the weather is hot will be valued differently by individuals from butter today in Warwick when it is cold. So we must also distinguish goods by what we call the state of nature. The latter is a description of the environment which is independent of anyone's action.

So, we have finished up with a collection of goods each of which is distinguished from others by any one of the four attributes: physical description, location, date of delivery and state of nature obtaining. The postulate of complete markets now implies, for instance, that there is given to the individual, terms on which he can trade butter in Warwick tomorrow if cold, bread in Warwick today when it is hot. That is, every good, as defined, has a price and so a market on which it is traded. The postulate is quite crucial for some of the claims made on behalf of the invisible hand, and its rejection has far-reaching consequences.

The decision units — agents, as we, alas, call them — are now divided into two groups: households and firms. The latter are owned by households and, in the pure theory, the managers of firms, in making decisions of what and how much to produce with what inputs, will act to maximize profits at prevailing prices, which is exactly what shareholders will want them to do. This again is a consequence of the complete market hypothesis, which ensures that uncertainty has been eliminated from the production decision, since markets permit complete insurance. This quite counterfactual implication I shall take up again later. I now add that each firm is supposed to have available to it a 'book of blueprints', that is, a list of input–output activities which are technologically feasible.

Households decide on trades including the trade in leisure they are endowed with. They are assumed to have a preference ranking over all possible trades, that is, they can decide which of two trading activities they prefer or which they are indifferent between. This ranking is consistent so that it never happens that trade A is preferred to trade B, and trade B to trade C, and trade C to trade A. Given all prices and the households' ownership of goods, leisure and shares of firms, we can deduce the set of trades which is market-feasible for the household. Any trade in that set has the property that expenditure on purchases does not exceed earnings from sales. Notice that borrowing and lending are included in this description. For instance, one borrows by selling a good (or money) for future delivery and one lends by buying a good (or money) for future delivery. Insurance is also included by the hypothesis that there are contingent future markets. Thus it is possible to make a contract for the delivery of goods in the future if the state of the world is that one is sick, and no delivery if one is well. It is now assumed that the household will choose a trade such that there is no other market-feasible trade which it prefers to the chosen one.

Given the ownership of goods and shares and the available books of blueprints, each agent will make a decision which is best for it on the basis of existing prices — the decision thus depends on prices only. We now come to the first question concerning the invisible hand. There clearly is no reason why, for an arbitrary set of prices, the multitude of decisions, taken by each agent in the light of his own motives only, should be consistent. By this I mean that there is no reason why, at arbitrary prices, trades should balance so that the amount of anything offered for sale is equal to what is demanded for purchase. However, it was proved in the 1950s that under certain conditions there always exists at least one set of economically meaningful non-negative prices at which the decisions arrived at individually will just mesh — that is, are consistent.

Whatever criticism I shall level at the theory later, I should like to record that it is a major intellectual achievement. One must be far gone in philistine turpitude not to appreciate the quite surprising nature of this result, or to be unmoved by the elegant means by which it is proved. It establishes the astonishing claim that it is logically possible to describe an economy in which millions of agents, looking no further than their own interests and responding to the spare information system of prices only, can none the less attain a coherent economic disposition of resources. Having made that clear, let me none the less emphasize the phrase 'logically possible'. Nothing whatever has been said of whether it is possible to describe any actual economy in these terms.

However, there is more to come. It can be shown under certain conditions that the allocation of goods achieved at the prices which lead to consistent choices — let us call them equilibrium prices — is such that there is no reallocation of goods between households possible which they all prefer to the allocation they have in equilibrium. Any reallocation must lead at least one household to a bundle to which the equilibrium bundle is preferred. We say that the equilibrium allocation is *Pareto-efficient*. But we can also establish a deeper and potentially much more useful result. Suppose the Cabinet decides on some Pareto-efficient allocation. If it is fully informed it would be rather foolish of it to decide on some allocation which is not Pareto-efficient, since it would gratuitously miss the opportunity of allowing all its citizens to reach a position which they prefer. Then it can be shown (again under certain conditions) that, provided it can impose any desired distribution of the ownership of goods among its citizens, there is one such distribution which, if it obtained in the unplanned economy, would lead the latter to reach an equilibrium allocation which coincides with the allocation the Cabinet had chosen. That is every Pareto-efficient allocation can be decentralized — handed over to the invisible hand. These two results are known as the Fundamental Theorems of Welfare Economics. They have led many to claim that the invisible hand is not only smart but also benificent. However, we notice at once that the benificence is somewhat limited. For there are many Pareto-efficient allocations and each one of them will have a different distribution of welfare. Mrs Thatcher's choice of a Pareto-efficient allocation, for instance, seems unlikely to correspond to any acceptable notion of distributive justice. Mr Benn's choice, on the other hand, may not even be Pareto-efficient. In any case, the sloppy habit in the literature in speaking of a Pareto-*optimum* has misled many people into believing that their duty of serious moral argument has been fulfilled when they can show that some policy outcome is Pareto-efficient. As a matter of fact, this is just the beginning of such an argument.

We can now look at some (by by no means all) of the limitations on the basic results which I have so far encapsulated in the phrase 'under certain conditions'. These limitations are separate from, and additional to, those which I shall discuss when I turn to the descriptive power of the pure theory. To make this clear I shall now discuss logical limitations.

Logical limitations of the pure theory

The whole theory is at risk if there are increasing returns which are 'large relative to the size of the economy'. This last phrase can be made precise but I shall not do that here. This risk is not only due to the circumstance that large increasing returns are usually associated with large firms and, hence, monopoly power, which is excluded by the hypothesis that agents take prices as beyond their control. It arises from the fact that, even if firms continued to act as price-takers, there may exist no equilibrium prices. Again I shall not document this. But it is clear that this logical limitation may, itself, rule out an appeal to the theory in concrete instances. If, however, an equilibrium exists it will again be Pareto-efficient, while it is no longer true that every Pareto-efficient allocation can be decentralized. So, even in the world of pure theory, the invisible hand may falter and such market outcomes as appear may be unsatisfactory, since they may have to involve monopolistic elements.

But this remark leads to a deeper problem. The theory has a lively sense of original sin — all people act entirely in their self-interest, quite narrowly defined. But, if that is so, will not individuals or groups of individuals seek to find ways to exert market power? By market power I mean a situation in which an individual's action can influence equilibrium prices. How can we be sure that the hypothesis that individuals act as if prices were given is not in conflict with the postulate that they are rational self-seeking agents? The answer is that we can only be sure if there is no market power for individuals to exploit. This can be shown to entail the condition that everyone in the economy, other than a given agent, can do as well when that agent trades as when he does not; this must be so whoever the given agent is. In general, this 'no surplus' condition will only be satisfied in 'large' economies. That is, in economies in which, in counting agents, we reckon any one individual as we would a single point in a collection of points on a continuous line — that is not at all. Of course, one can rest satisfied if this is approximately true. But once again the purely logical limitations of the theory will restrict its range of applicability.

When market power is present the Smithian vision of the invisible hand is lost. Instead of the machine-like responses of agents to prices, the agents will find themselves engaged in a game. That is, it will be necessary for them to take account of the decisions of other agents and, in particular, they may have to consider how these decisions are affected by their own. Their choices will now be among strategies. Here economists are not agreed even what the appropriate notion of an equilibrium should be. But it becomes easy to show that plausible equilibria are no longer Pareto-efficient. Moreover, it has not been established that all plausible notions are non-vacuous, that is, that they are logically possible. In short, there is no accepted theory of the invisible hand when the no-surplus condition is not satisfied.

One must conclude that one cannot invoke the classical theory of the invisible hand in dealing with economies in which agents have market power. If such an economy attains some coherent state to be called 'equilibrium' all market information will not be summarised by prices. The signals to which agents respond will be much richer and the kind of things they would like to know, in order to arrive at decisions, much more varied. One can, however, assert that outcome will, in general, not be Pareto-efficient.

I have already noted that the complete market hypothesis is crucial and also counterfactual. Here, I want to draw attention to a purely logical difficulty which on reflection has rather wide implications. Two agents cannot enter into a contract in which delivery is contingent on an event which they cannot both observe. For, certainly, our greedy agents do not trust each other. Hence, if information differs between agents, certain contingent markets cannot exist as a matter of logic. This was first noticed by Radner.[1]

Now that we have considered the possibility of differences in information, all sorts of other problems arise. Recall that we distinguished goods by, among other things, their physical description. What exactly is the physical description of a second-hand motor car or, for that matter, any of the multitudinous objects which we use and whose properties we know nothing about? Similar problems arise in the market for labour and insurance markets. In all these cases, agents on one side of the market have information which is superior to that possessed by agents on the other. The role of prices now becomes much more complex. In particular, prices will induce 'sorting' or 'selection' and they may also serve to transfer some of the information of the informed to the uninformed. For instance, in certain cases, not yet fully explored, the prices of a class of goods may be correlated positively with their quality and so serve as a sign of quality.

There are many difficult and interesting problems here which, at the level of the whole economy, have only been partially resolved. One thing is clear: in such situations the set of signals is again likely to be larger than that consisting only of prices. Thus, for instance, educational qualifications will be used to signal one's quality to prospective employers. Once again the Fundamental Theorems of Welfare Economics will fail. This brings me to the last two of the logical limitations of the pure theory which I shall take up.

Information can be acquired by expanding resources but, once one has it, it is not diminished if someone else has it as well. It is an example of a public good. For quite obvious reasons the Fundamental Welfare Theorems cannot hold when there are public goods. Indeed, the market economy will perform disastrously in such cases. No one will invest in the production of information if its market price is necessarily zero. That is why we have patent and copyright laws. Such devices are forced on us by the logic of the invisible hand. Of course, there are many other examples of public goods.

In the example of the education signal of my quality it will be clear that the effectiveness of my signal will depend on the signals used by others. There is here what we call an *externality* — that is, an effect of one agent's action on the welfare of another. There are many cases of externalities, both positive and negative. But this is so well known, and the failure of the invisible hand in such situations so widely understood, that I will not dwell on them. I only want to make one observation inspired by some recent work by Makowski.[2] If the 'no-surplus' condition is not met there must be an externality, almost by definition; that means that externalities are implicit in any departure from perfect competition. This seems to imply that one cannot ascribe failures of the invisible hand in the face of externalities exclusively to defective property rights. In any case, ever since Marshall and Pigou it has been agreed that externalities constitute a prima-facie case for government intervention in a market economy. Hence, economies which significantly depart from perfect competition — that, is, in general, actual economies — would be candidates for the deployment of a visible hand.

This brings me to Fred Hirsch's famous book *The Social Limits of Growth*,[3] where he considers the obstacles in the way of the invisible hand occasioned by non-augmentable 'social' or 'positional' goods. A simple and old example is the case of a common pasture where what your cow eats reduces what is available for mine. Another example is congestion on a motorway or in a beauty spot. In general, these are cases of externalities.

For many such cases corrections can be achieved without essential damage to the price mechanism. This can be done by a levying of suitable taxes and subsidies and by the creation of appropriate property rights. In some cases one may have to impose direct controls. But, even here, the price system can be utilized, for instance, a licensing arrangement with tradable licences. On the other hand, there are externalities, and these are the ones which preoccupied Hirsch, where the only remedy appears to lie in changing what people want. For instance, as Gilbert and Sullivan remind us, there may be no way to satisfy everyone's desire to be 'somebody'. If we all desire to dine in exclusive restaurants this cannot be met entirely by giving us all equal access. The externality of envy is perhaps also only correctible when there is nothing to envy.

Hirsch considers these matters to be a source of what Marx would have called 'contradiction'. In the early stages of a market economy most people are concerned with eminently reproducible necessities of life. The invisible hand works in harmony with expectations and leads to the growth in the output of goods which people desire. At a later and more materially opulent stage people develop wants for goods which are intrinsically non-augmentable and thus become increasingly concerned with positional goods. Their expectations are then bound to be disappointed and disappointment will lead to disaffection. The invisible hand cannot provide what people desire. The sum total of human happiness can now only continue to increase by a change in what makes people happy. In particular, greed and the desire for self-advancement must give way to the gentler social virtues of affection and co-operation. But these virtues are not consistent with the motives which provide power to the invisible hand. The intrinsic limitations in the supply of those things which capitalist economies come to desire most must essentially herald the end of that particular social arrangement.

Clearly, here is an important and interesting point. But I must confess to some discomfort with theorizing on such a grand and ominous scale. For instance, it is not clear beyond doubt that the limits which Hirsch has in mind are absolute. To put it differently, Hirsch may have underestimated the availability of substitutes. For example, while we cannot all enjoy comparative solitude in the same beauty spot, we may be able to do so in our garden. While we cannot all be equally esteemed as musicians or mathematicians, we can multiply almost endlessly the activities which provide opportunities to be esteemed. Moreover, one of the fruits of growth is the increase in leisure and I am unconvinced that there are intrinsic limitations to its benificence. Lastly, the purely physical inventiveness of the system sees to it that we continue to have a healthy appetite for augmentable goods. What self-respecting person does not now desire a video-tape recorder? In short, I think that Hirsch has undoubtedly shown that externalities in the most general sense are more pervasive and sometimes more intractable than had often been supposed. To that extent, he has diminished the scope of the invisible hand and enlarged that of collective action. It remains to be seen whether he has discovered a poison that will kill the hand altogether.

Adam Smith and John Stuart Mill, to name only two classical exponents of the invisible hand theory, were certainly aware of some of the limitations of the efficacy of the market. Indeed, they used these to formulate a theory of the legitimate, or at least appropriate, sphere of action of governments. But they and many of their modern successors undoubtedly underestimate the extent of the ground that has to be yielded. Moreover, their line of argument runs into another danger. To demonstrate the logical possibility of market failure, indeed to demonstrate that such failure actually occurs on a large scale, is not in itself a demonstration of the desirability of government intervention. For market failure is not a necessary ground for intervention — the market outcome may be associated with great injustice even where there is no failure. Nor is such failure sufficient grounds for intervention, since it remains to be demonstrated that 'government failure' is less damaging than market failure. Hence, while there may be a prima-facie ground for intervention when the invisible hand fails, and no such grounds when it does not, there is some arguing and thinking to be done before a case for intervention has been clinched. But before I do some of this arguing I now want to consider — however briefly and superficially — some of the descriptive limitations of the pure theory.

The descriptive limitations of the pure theory

I have already mentioned the logical grounds which arise from the circumstance that markets may be incomplete. I now notice that, as a matter of plain fact, they *are* incomplete. The proof is readily at hand: we observe that there is trading at every date, which would not be the case in a complete market world. In fact, the complete market hypothesis is convincingly falsified.

But economists and particularly theoretical economists do not give up easily. Granted that markets are incomplete, is it possible that (a) the theory has made unnecessarily strong assumptions in asking for complete markets and (b) that there are considerations not depending on all markets existing which allow the pure theory to look the facts in the face and continue serenely on its way?

As an example, suppose there are only two physically distinct goods and only one date and location to consider. Let there be five possible states of the world. Then the complete market hypothesis suggests that we need two times five, that is, ten markets. But Arrow[4] noted that whatever allocation might be achieved by ten markets could also be achieved by seven. That is two markets for the two goods and five markets for securities, each one of which would pay something positive in one of the states and nothing in the other four. An individual can always find a trade in these seven markets which allows him to do as well as by trading in ten. So the pure theory does make stronger assumption than it needs. But one can assert with confidence that even the reduced number of markets suggested by Arrow is much larger than the number of markets which we observe. This is clear when we think of many future dates and states.

Recently, Bewley[5] has suggested that the holding of money balances can, in certain circumstances, provide almost all the insurance possibilities afforded by complete markets. His analysis is very impressive but I believe he would agree that it is impossible to claim that it applies to actual economies.

The second line of defence involves the invocation of 'rational expectations', a move widely favoured at present. By rational expectations one means that individuals who, because of incomplete markets, now have to form market expectations do so by using all the information available to them and do so consistently. The notion of an equilibrium is enlarged: not only must markets clear and individuals do as well for themselves as they can, but also there must be no systematic falsification of rationally formed expectations. The new concept has been christened *rational expectations equilibrium*. It has been vastly influential, especially with people who would not find it easy to really understand the idea. For instance, the view that inflation can have no permanent effect on employment or that monetary policy has no real consequences even in the short term, if rationally anticipated, is based on the rational expectations hypothesis. As empirical evidence one can point to the result that prices of securities traded on the stock exchange perform a random walk, which is consistent with the theory that the price of any security reflects all the information which can be rationally comprehended plus a random error term which cannot.

The first point to make now is that this move does not re-establish the benificence of the invisible hand: rational expectations equilibria need not be Pareto-efficient. Indeed, there seem in general to be many rational expectations equilibria and it is possible that some of these can be Pareto-ranked. Secondly, while the theory points in at least one right direction — namely that systematic errors in expectations will lead to the revision of those expectations — it is hard to consider this new equilibrium as descriptively satisfactory. For instance, to make it consistent with our observation of fluctuations in real magnitudes like employment and output, its proponents have had to resort to *ad hoc* postulates of mistakes rationally made. They often argue that it is government policy which induces people to make such mistakes. For example, unknowable or unobservable changes in the money supply will cause people to confuse price changes caused by 'real' events and those which are purely nominal. But introspection and observation suggest that we are quite capable of making mistakes unaided. More importantly, most people do not have sufficiently well-formulated forecasts to allow them to be mistaken in the first place. Thus, we all make some sort of guess at the inflation rate but few are sufficiently coherent and patient to form a probability distribution over such rates, nor are we clever enough to use correctly all the information at our disposal. If we lived in an essentially stationary environment and if we lived long enough, or knew history well enough, we might none the less come close to satisfying the postulates of the theory. But we do not.

The rational expectations approach has its theoretical uses. It allows us to examine economies free from expectational disturbances and perhaps isolate other sources of ill behaviour. It permits us to show that even in such a world the invisible hand may cease to guide before it has made citizens as well off as, in the given circumstances, they could be. It also allows us to sidestep an issue which is enveloped in ignorance, namely how expectations are actually formed. But people who base policies for real economies on the belief that citizens form their expectations rationally and that the invisible hand, if left to its own devices, will guide us to a rational expectations equilibrium with not much delay cannot, I think, be taken seriously. By this I mean that I consider the direct evidence overwhelmingly against this view and I regard the 'as if' evidence from such econometric models as there are, as I do evidence for miracles: the story is simply too much at variance with experience.

However, we should notice a spin-off from this approach which is at once obvious and important. In forming their expectations, in whatever manner and however imperfectly people do form them, account will be taken of expected government policy. An act of policy which has been more or less foreseen will, in general, have different consequences from one which has not. This not very deep observation has often been neglected in discussions of economic policy. In analysis it can give rise to some tricky and interesting problems. Rational expectations theorists, although they have characteristically embraced rather extreme models, have none the less made an important contribution in making everyone aware of this consideration.

In so far as rational expectations are descriptively unsatisfactory, we would expect the invisible hand to falter and, perhaps, to mislead its actual intertemporal operations. For instance, speculative bubbles which eventually burst are possible. That such bubbles have been observed can be shown to be evidence against rational expectations. Quite generally, there is no logical obstacle to an economy pursuing a path which runs into feasibility constraints and so experiences discontinuous dislocation. It is not unimportant that this should be more widely understood than seems, at present, to be the case. I shall, therefore, make the same point again in a slightly different form.

If the invisible hand is to operate there must be sufficient opportunities for intertemporal and contingent intertemporal trade. In fact there are not enough of these opportunities. The lack of contingent markets means that the market economy is associated with more uncertainty than pure theory allows. The lack of intertemporal markets means that great weight must rest on market expectations. The rational expectations hypothesis substitutes an internal and psychic hand for the market. Each individual somehow has learned how the invisible hand would have performed if it had been given markets in which to perform. If it is agreed that this is not of high descriptive merit, there is, in fact, no obvious mechanism by which intertemporal decisions can be co-ordinated. This was Keynes's view. I have yet to see it refuted. The French drew the conclusion that they at least required indicative planning. The Japanese have for a long time employed non-market institutions to supplement private investment decisions. In West Germany, the banks seem to act as market substitutes. In Britain, where politicians now follow gurus rather than arguments, we are all set to rely on the invisible hand doing a job which, in practice, it will not and cannot do.

The other large misfit between the pure theory and the world in which I have already noted under the heading of logical limitations is, of course, the postulate of perfect competition, that is, the assumption that economic agents know all they need to know when they know prices. That this is false many observations confirm. Advertising and market research, trade unions and market-sharing arrangements, and expensive business investigations to forecast demand are just a few of the falsifiers. The theoretical consequence of this misfit is that even when a coherent disposition of resources is achieved, one will not be able to claim that it is Pareto-efficient. That is, in general, one can describe some form of collective or co-operative action which would improve the lot of everyone. But I will not now pursue further this quite important scene, for there are still many more central issues to be discussed.

The invisible hand in motion

So far I have considered only situations in which the invisible hand has already accomplished its task. That is, I have been concerned with equilibrium states. But that must be no more than half the story. Suppose, for instance, it is possible for an egg to stay standing on its tip until it is disturbed. We should not attach great practical significance to this equilibrium in the egg until we were told some causal story of how it comes to be in that state. In exactly the same way, the proposition that, in certain circumstances, there is a set of prices which ensures equality between demand and supply in all markets tells us nothing of whether these prices will indeed be established by a market economy. On this central question neither economic theory nor evidence is at all satisfactory.

Before I enlarge on this I want to stress what a significant lacuna this represents and the danger in its being ignored by policy advocates. Seeing our ignorance, a number of Chicago and other economists have decided that the best way to proceed is to pretend that is is not really there. This they do with the aid of some pseudo-philosophical remarks concerning the meaning of equilibrium and the autonomy of human action. In any case, they simply assume that the invisible hand performs its task instantaneously and, as it were, superinvisibly. Thus, for these economists, wages at any moment of time have just those values which, given other prices, ensure that everyone willing to work finds a willing employer. This is not a theory, or a deduction from a theory, but an axiom. Fluctuations in employment are then explained by the expectational errors which I have already discussed. For instance, Britain's unemployed workers are without a job because, at the going wage, they do not want one. They do not want one because either they prefer subsidised idleness or they expect real wages to rise and are thus trading present for future leisure. On the basis of this specious nonsense Keynes has been pronounced dead and Mrs Thatcher advised.

Although I am sure this is nonsense as descriptive economics, I am, as a theorist, more concerned with the intellectual move which axiomatically ensures that the invisible hand is never observed in reconciling inconsistent plans and so provides no account of how it might actually do this. It seems clear that this leaves the theory essentially incomplete. It also seems obvious that it cannot be usefully confronted with other theories, for it is no answer to the Keynesian proposition that there may be states in which willing workers cannot find a job at the going wage to announce it as an axiom that this can never happen.

Less extreme theories have recognized that some story must be told and to the non-economist the chosen one is known as the 'law of supply and demand'. Here the invisible hand is actually set in motion. When demand for anything exceeds its supply the price will go up, and vice versa when supply exceeds demand. In taking this account seriously, one finds oneself studying a rather complex dynamic system. It is a fact that this study has not led to the conclusion that this behaviour of prices must guide the economy to its tranquil equilibrium. Indeed, almost the converse is true: only very special assumptions seem to ensure this happy outcome.

But this may be so because we have not told a correct story. Great difficulties are encountered in this undertaking when one insists on retaining the perfect competition hypothesis. For strictly speaking, there is no one agent who can actually be taken to do the price changing. Largely for this reason the analysis has followed Walras in postulating a fictional auctioneer whose task is to adjust prices in accordance with 'the law of demand'. But while there are auction markets in actual economies they are pretty rare and it is not at all clear what real process the fictional auctioneer represents. If, however, we recognize that actual agents are involved in changing prices because they have transitory or permanent market power we shall also start to get a grip on the theory by exploiting the very basic axiom that agents are out to improve themselves. This kind of analysis is in its infancy and there are no general results to report.

But certain rather important implications of this unsatisfactory approach can be observed. During the process individuals will not only encounter prices but also trading experiences which will influence their subsequent actions. If you find that the baker is frequently out of bread you may buy crackers instead. If the baker, in turn, is slow to notice that he has unsatisfied customers he may never notice it, because in the meantime they have gone to the cracker shop. If there are workers who cannot find a job, this will affect what they can buy and so the job prospects and actions of others. Employers noticing the unemployed willing workers may find it profitable to lower wages. On the other hand, they may not since this might lead existing trained workers to leave or to strike, or the firm may fear for its reputation as a good employer. It may also not be possible, for reasons to be explained by a theory of implicit labour contracts, to pay new workers less than existing ones. But, in spite of all this, money wages may indeed fall. However, since the demand signals were unfavourable, it is not at all certain that employment will rise. The analysis of the process is hazardous even in ruthlessly simplified models and not at all always favourable to the invisible hand.

In particular, there is now a possibility that the invisible hand may cease to move before its task is accomplished — I have elsewhere referred to this as the hand getting stuck. For if price changes are the outcome of the calculations of actual participants in the economy, they may certainly be miscalculated. That is, the participants may judge the price change not to be to their advantage when it really is. But even when they calculate correctly this may happen. For the consequences to you of your price change depend on the calculations of others as to the consequences to be expected from their price change in turn. Keynesians refer to such situations as bootstrap situations. A given employer's willingness to lower wages and a potential employee's willingness to accept the job on these terms will not be independent of whether other employers have calculated it to be to their advantage to lower the wage or, as Negishi[6] has noted, a worker who would be willing to work at a wage below that ruling may none the less correctly calculate that the effect of lowering his wage on the probability of finding a job is too small to make it worthwhile.

While I want to re-emphasize that these are all possibilities in particular constructions rather than general propositions, I feel confident enough to conjecture that very shortly a very large and rigorous collection of models with these possibilities will be available. In game theory we are quite familiar with the notion of multiple equilibria and with the insight that co-operative solutions may dominate non-co-operative ones. The paths which I am now indicating are much more familiar to game theorists than they are to orthodox pure theorists.

Of course, there is a great deal more to say on this matter but I can allow myself only one more observation. The pure market proponents sometimes argue against the possibilities which I have just described by noting that they would result in there being unexploited gains to trade. This they regard as inconsistent with a world of rational agents. In this last view I consider them to be profoundly mistaken. Opportunities for mutually advantageous trade must be recognised and hence signalled. We can imagine a world where groups of individuals bump into each other at random and proceed to explore the possibility of trade. It is not our world and it is not the world under discussion. In that world, trade opportunities are supposedly signalled by prices which are public and anonymous — they do not depend on persons engaged in the trade. Of course, there are exceptions to this but the theory under review does not consider these. In such a world, it is false to propose that, because there are unexploited gains from trade, it will always be rational to signal this by price changes. The manner in which potential traders can communicate is basic significance. One should have thought that, in an age where the prisoner's dilemma is known far and wide, this point hardly needed making.

Some general remarks and some tentative conclusions

I have for much of the time been arguing that the emperor's clothes are not quite as fine as is often supposed. Although I have not been as precise and detailed as a more leisurely account would have permitted, I none the less hope to have shown that, on purely logical considerations as well as on the basis of quite simple observations, the invisible hand is likely to be unsure in its operation and occasionally downright arthritic. However, as I have already warned, it is an unwarranted inference from this that there is some social device which will perform satisfactorily or that we should cut off the hand altogether.

One of the reasons for the failings of the invisible hand, at least in theory, is that the task assigned to it is extremely complex. This task will not go away when, for instance, we propose to replace the market by the planner. In this connection Professor Hayek, whose doctrines on many economic matters I do not consider sound, made a very important one. He argued that economically relevant information was highly decentralized. A professional cook, for instance, will know more about the dishes he could prepare from a chicken and be better informed of his customers' tastes than would a plumber or an economist. Indeed, it is quite clear that such specialized knowledge and information is commonplace. Now one of the claims made for the price system by Hayek was that it successfully aggregates this information so that the economy behaves as if there had been no specialized knowledge in the first place. Hayek did not prove this to be so and it is only very recently that we have understood the circumstances in which the claim made is correct.

I will not now discuss this particular issue in that particular way, if for no other reason than that the matter is quite technical. However, we do not need to do that in order to see the force of Hayek's point that any planner must find means to utilize and to aggregate the private information of citizens. Even when the invisible hand performs the task imperfectly it does perform it after some fashion. It is not at all clear in what fashion it could be performed without the price system altogether. This may be the reason why so many socialist economies have progressively allowed the invisible hand to regain some of its old importance.

The economizing of information and the utilization of widely dispersed information is one feature of a market economy which has only recently been studied with the seriousness it deserves. It is already evident that the outcome will not always be as good as it could have been if an all-knowing agent were in control. It also seems possible that a more limited agent could nudge the system to prevent it settling on unsatisfactory or downright bad outcomes. But no discussion of a planned economy begins to tackle the issues seriously when it ignores these informational tasks. Certainly, the literature on economic planning has for a good time been aware of this and, also, of other potential virtues of the price system. Indeed, sometimes the pure theory which I have outlined is not taken descriptively but prescriptively. That is, the task of the planners is to make the invisible hand work as the textbook says it does: for instance, by instructing functionaries to follow marginal cost pricing rules or to attain some prescribed rate of return in their investment plans.

But this leads naturally to another problem which I have already touched upon in my discussion of Hirsch. In so far as the invisible hand moves it is moved by greed. To buy in the cheapest and sell in the dearest market, to change job to earn a higher wage, to raise prices to tap some of the surplus from unsatisfied buyers, these are all virtues for the market system. If business managers were to take decisions in the light of what they perceive to be their 'social responsibility', or if, in general, agents were to value the welfare of others outside their family at all seriously, the invisible hand might still do this and that, but it would cease to do what Adam Smith claimed for it. This to many people is an unattractive feature of the hand, though I incline to the Johnsonian view that a man is, in normal times, rather innocently engaged when he is making money. But that is evidently contentious. What I believe is not so is the insight that the market system operates on relatively simple motivational precepts which, in principle, leave agents open to manipulation by authority, while substitute systems are partly unfathomable because they leave the motives of the actors nebulous. Once again, the history of socialist countries suggests that the dislike of bourgeois greed has frequently had to give way to the necessity of providing coherent and appealing motives for people to do what is wanted. Kornai[7] has given an interesting account of how greed can be replaced by apathy and lassitude when greed has nothing to bite on, and of how unsatisfactory this proved to be in Hungary. In any case, to ask individuals or groups of individuals to act 'in the common interest' is, except in well-defined exceptional cases, not to ask anything comprehensible of them at all.

Of course the market system not only allocates resources, it also powerfully influences the distribution of the enjoyment of resources among individuals. The Fundamental Theorems of Welfare Economics suggest that to some extent one should be able to divorce these two sides of the same coin. In fact we know that, even in our most simplified models, this cannot, in general, be perfectly done: one may have to make trades between equity and efficiency. Pigou noted this over 50 years ago, and his arguments have since been refined without being altered in their essentials. The actual terms of such a trade are not really known. Greed may take many forms. For instance, it may be satisfied by rewards which, while they exceed one's neighbour's reward, do so only slightly. This is what Keynes believed, and he thought that the greed game could be played successfully for much smaller stakes. No one knows whether he was right. But this question will arise whatever the mode of economic organization — if one wants people to act in a certain way one must give them a reason for doing so.

At this stage, it is proper to note an objection in the manner in which I have dealt with the market economy. Many people will argue that the allocative role of a market economy is not by any means the most important role. Rather it is the opportunities which it affords for innovation and ingenuity and for the risk-taking entrepreneur and thus for growth in welfare. It was Schumpeter, rather than Walras, who saw down to the essence of things and it was Keynes on animal spirits, rather than Arrow–Debreu on general equilibrium, who understood the motor in the capitalist machine. On this view, obstacles placed in the path of greed and self-advancement, such as result from an egalitarian public finance, are liable to have consequences much more serious than 'just a misallocation of resources'. Such obstacles may lead to stagnation or continuous decline. Moreover, proponents of this view will argue that there is no substitute for the hero in the market. Civil servants are not readily cast in the mould of captains of industry or that of Schumpeterian innovators.

My first comment on this view is defensive. The critics are not right when they suggest that the market theory is not relevant to the story of growth. In fact, that theory is just as much concerned with the *inter*temporal, as it is with the *intra*temporal, allocation of resources. For instance, it is highly relevant to the understanding of the investment–consumption choice, which in turn is very near the centre of an understanding of processes of growth. It is simply a mistake to believe that the equilibrium which I have discussed is bound to be stationary or even quasi-stationary.

My second comment is that, none the less, the critics have a point. Certainly, economic theory does not provide an answer to Weber's famous question why Britain rather than China should have been the first to have an Industrial Revolution. Nor, indeed, has economic theory helped much in accounting for the Japanese post-war sprint or for the relative British decline. Plainly there are here crucial elements which go beyond market signals and market behaviour. On these grand matters economics is comparatively silent.

But it is not entirely mute either. To take an example, recent studies, based on the traditional view of market choice, have much illuminated the relation between market structure and R & D expenditure. Such expenditures are undertaken with peculiarly uncertain outcomes; they are part and parcel of competitive battles and they are likely, because of the operation of the law of large numbers, to be subject to significant increasing returns. Oligopolistic industries will, in this area, take decisions which differ from those of monopolistic or competitive ones and we can actually pin down that difference. Similar insights have been gained on the question of what are the main determinants of the adoption of inventions, once made. In all of this the invisible hand plays a part in guiding the direction of innovative activity. I need only remind you of the effects of the rise in the real price of oil on motorcar design to make the point obvious. Moreover, there are good reasons to suppose that the invisible hand will work imperfectly. This is partly due to the increasing returns and to the public good aspect of invention and discovery. The theory also suggests some ways in which these failures can at least be rendered smaller with market-using policies.

However, many people have a liking for grand questions and some of them have been arguing that economics should give way to political economy. Sometimes that is a disguised invitation to enter the claustrophobic world of Marx, often it is a plea for 'universal social science'. The latter is not a self-evidently plausible project. If it is, then it will certainly require a genius which makes such advice unhelpful. At its best, the invitation is to look circumspectly and in a precise manner a little beyond traditional boundaries. Hirsch has shown that this can be fruitful.

But we should not, I think, be surprised by our large areas of ignorance. Indeed, I would find it more surprising if there were available or possible a total theory of history and society. Such theories as have been proposed are pretty clearly bogus. The questions of the theory which I have been propounding are more modest and more useful. In the first instance, it is a powerful test for organizing one's thought and for detecting unsound arguments. For example, the insight that the pursuit of self-interest need not have undesirable social consequences, as well as a precise account of the case where it does do so, is of great utility. Should fisheries be left to the market? Do we need an energy policy? Should the poor be aided by rent control? In these and hundreds of other instances the theory is not only the most powerful but also the only available means by which we can attain coherence of argument. Robertson thought that benevolence was one of the scarcest of goods and that it should therefore be demanded only sparingly. Many politicians propose programmes which suppose that it is a free good. It is a great virtue of the theory that it suggests ways in which institutions and policies might be devised, which harness self-interest and render it socially acceptable. It thus allows one to proceed while humanity is what it seems to be.

At the end of all this there is no crisp and clear final reckoning. The limitations on the applicability of pure market theory are numerous and some of them are quite serious. The exceptions to the benificence of the invisible hand have been piling up since Adam Smith and, much later, Pigou considered them. Our knowledge of the actual movements of the hand is rudimentary and vastly incomplete. The increase of market power of all kinds has produced formidable conceptual problems in the construction of theories. The Smithsonian vision still provides a reference point but an increasingly remote one. It can also be dangerously misleading when this limited role is not recognized. This, as I have argued, is illustrated by some recent American writings on the relation of wages and employment and is further exemplified by the exponents of supply economics. All these advocates say much more than even the pure theory allows them to say, and infinitely more than the applicability of that theory permits. Although Mrs Thatcher has recently denied vehemently that her policies are based on any economic theory, that is, that the policies have coherent origins — this must not be taken at its face value! She has, after all, diagnosed unique cures for our ills, and in her pronouncements the Smithian hand is quite visible.

The predominant conclusion must be that we are quite certain of what really is the case. The pretence that it is otherwise comes under the heading of religion or magic. Once the uncertainty is recognised it will greatly affect the set of rational or reasonable actions. Traditional theory is quite powerful on the question of the control of systems which are imperfectly understood. It suggests that, exceptional and near-catastrophic circumstances apart, it will not in general be wise to put all your eggs in one basket or to give harsh pulls on levers. That is, unless you are what economists call a risk-lover. But risk-loving itself is unreasonable. In any case, these are the reasons why, as I said at the outset, the wishy-washy, step-by-step, case-by-case approach seems to me to be the only reasonable one in economic policy.

But many people, to my surprise, prefer to go out with a bang rather than a whimper. Very few people can live with a shadowy and ill-defined picture of our world. So I place no bets on the reasonable approach winning through. In this country it is very likely that the non-fulfilment of the vastly exaggerated claims for the invisible hand will lead to a reaction in which the hand, to our great loss, will be amputated forever. The age of prophets and of witches is upon us and such an age is not friendly to reason.

Notes

1. R. Radner. 'Competition Equilibrium under Uncertainty', *Econometrica*, vol. 38, 1968.
2. L. Makowski, 'The Characterization of Perfect Competition', *Journal of Economic Theory*, 1980.
3. Fred Hirsch, *The Social Limits to Growth*, London, 1977.
4. K.J. Arrow, 'The Role of Securities in the Optimal Allocation of Risk-Bearing', *Review of Economic Studies*, vol. 31, 1963.
5. T. Bewley, 'The Optimum Quantity of Money' in J. Kareken and N. Wallace (eds), *Federal Reserve Bank of Minnesota*, 1980.
6. T. Negishi, 'Existence of an Underemployment Equilibrium' in Schwödiauer (ed.) *Equilibrium and Disequilibrium in Economic Theory*, Dordrecht, 1974.
7. J. Kornai, *Anti-Equilibrium*, Amsterdam, 1971.

7 The profit motive

Amartya Sen

In an important and influential paper called 'The Results of Human Action but not of Human Design', Friedrich von Hayek has noted the limitations of those theories — economic, political, legal or whatever — that have 'no room for anything which is "the result of human action but not of human design"'.[1] In this context, Hayek pays particular attention to the achievements of self-seeking and profit maximization — producing public good through private motivation — and argues against the alleged virtues of 'deliberate design and planning'. He complains, with justice, about 'the uncomprehending ridicule' later poured on Adam Smith's 'expression of the "invisible hand" by which "man is led to promote an end which was not part of his intention"', and the consequent undermining of what Hayek calls 'this profound insight into the object of all social theory'.

However, all's well that ends well, and Hayek notes that the basic idea — revived by Carl Menger — 'now . . . seems to have become widely accepted, at least within the field of social theory proper'.[2] Certainly Adam Smith's version of it is now part of the standard tradition of economics. The professional economist is, by and large, much taken by the notion of private motivation achieving public good through the intermediary of the market mechanism. The results of two recent surveys of views of professional economists in the UK and the USA, analysed respectively by Samuel Brittan,[3] and Kearl, Pope, Whiting and Wimmer,[4] bring out the point forcefully,.

In the British survey, it is in fact also possible to compare the response of professional economists with those of Members of Parliament. It is interesting to note that a very much higher percentage of professional economists than Members of Parliament accepted the claim that 'in a free-enterprise economy, the presumed harmony between individual and public interest' is brought about by 'competitive markets and pursuit of self-interest by individuals' and/or 'a strong desire for profit maximization'.

Amartya Sen is Professor of Economics and Philosophy at Harvard University. This article is the text of the fourth Fred Hirsch Memorial Lecture given in Washington DC on 17 November 1982 at the Eugene R. Black Auditorium of the World Bank. It first appeared in *Lloyds Bank Review*, no. 147, January 1983.

It is perhaps more interesting to observe that while 79 per cent of professional economists accepted this claim the proportion of even *Conservative* MPs, not to mention the others, agreeing with that view was 20 per cent less than that figure, with a sizeable minority emphasizing the role of 'careful planning and coordination', and 'the exercise of social responsibility by private businessmen'.

Also rather interestingly, among the economists, the business economists were relatively the most sceptical of the claim. While 62 per cent of the business economists gave answers pinpointing markets, self-interest and profits, the proportions for academic economists and government economists were 82 per cent and 87 per cent respectively. The economists furthest from business had, it appears, the greatest respect for its ability to turn the pursuit of self-interest into a harmonious pursuance of public interest. Indeed, the academic economists who had devised the questionnaire had ticked the answer that the presumed harmony is brought about by 'competitive markets and pursuit of self-interest by individuals' as the 'correct' answer. One has to look only at standard textbooks to see the extent to which belief in that 'presumed harmony' and in that view of the correct answer is part of the basic training of the modern economist.

In this lecture I would like to re-examine the role of markets and self-seeking behaviour in achieving economic success. I would argue that the standard approach takes a remarkably limited view of the nature of the economic problem and of the tasks that an economy has to perform.

I am aware that there is a danger that the the examination of private motivation and public interest may look like an annual event associated with the name of Fred Hirsch. Professor Frank Hahn gave the third Fred Hirsch Memorial Lecture last year on the subject of 'Reflections of the Invisible Hand',[5] and he discussed with his characteristic clarity and elegance the economic theory of markets, and what self-seeking may or may not do in economic allocation. I am not daunted by the danger of asking much the same questions again, since the questions are important and also because I shall argue for a somewhat different reading of both the contents of the questions and, naturally, the answers that they call for. Also, I believe, it is not inappropriate to pay particular attention to the roles of self-interest and the invisible hand in a Fred Hirsch Memorial Lecture, since Fred Hirsch has done such outstanding work in this area. His *The Social Limits to Growth*[6] presents some of the most interesting and far-reaching arguments on this issue.

Intentions and results

The Hayekian claim regarding the profundity of the insight provided by the perspective of 'the results of human action but not of human design' seems to me to be difficult to sustain. That actions often have results different from and quite the opposite of their intended effects can, of course, be a matter of some significance. This possibility has been investigated in many different ways in social theory, one example being the Marxian study of dialectics, including the well-known argument that the actions of capitalists have the effect of ultimately destroying the system. Hayek himself has given several good examples of *contrariness* between design and outcome. It is, however, important to distinguish between those results of an action that are just not part of the design and those that are *opposite* to what was designed.

It is, I fear, a rather *un*profound thought to recognize that any action has many results that were not part of the design of the agent. This cannot but be the case. I cross the street at the pedestrian crossing, and this action has many results. First, I am now on the other side of the street, as indeed I intended to be. Second, you saw me crossing the street. Normally I would not give a damn whether you did or not, and almost certainly I did not have that vision of yours as part of my design. Third, I delayed a passing car slightly, which was not a part of my design. Fourth, the driver gets home slightly later; that was not my design. Fifth, the driver's delayed arrival makes the actions at his home slightly different in timing and possibly even in content. These things did not figure in my choice. If this discourse is generating boredom, then I have succeeded in making my point. The recognition that many results of our actions are not reflections of our design can, in itself, scarcely be one of great profundity.

It would be, of course, quite a different matter if the interesting results happened to be the *opposite* of what we intended. But it is important to recognize that this is not the case with the invisible hand, by which — in Adam Smith's words — 'man is led to promote an end which was no part of his intention'. It is certainly the case, as Adam Smith made clear, that 'it is not from the benevolence of the butcher, the brewer, or the baker that we expect our dinner, but from their regard to their own interest'.[7] But the butcher, the brewer and the baker did not have a design that we should starve — a design that got frustrated by their pursuit of it. The butcher and friends wanted to make money and so indeed they did. We intended to have dinner, as indeed we did. There is nothing startling or deeply illuminating in the recognition that not *all* results were part of the design of *every* agent.

Congruence and conflicts

The reason why this point is important is that the Smithian argument partly rests precisely on the ability of the market to *achieve* the results intended by individuals, that is, to fulfil the 'designs' of the participants

— and *then* some more. I want bread and will happily give some money for it, and the baker wants money and will give me a loaf of bread in exchange. When we carry out the exchange, we do achieve what we set out to achieve, and in the process we have helped each other. In more complex cases, too — with many agents and with production in addition to trade — the market works on the basis of congruence of interests of different participants. That is the essence of the Smithian perspective: different people have a common interest in exchange and the market gives them the opportunity to pursue their common interests — with success, *not* failure. Of course, they also have conflicting interests in many other matters, but the market is not concerned with resolving these conflicts.

It is precisely because the market equilibrium is partly what the agents designed to achieve that it has the various efficiency properties that fill up the textbooks on market achievements. The market, on that analysis, turns out to be quite a good way of having results of human action that are *also* of human design. Given certain assumptions — especially the absence of interdependences working outside the market (the so-called 'externalities') — every competitive equilibrium is Pareto-optimal, which means that no one can be made better off without making someone else worse off. Also, under certain — rather more stringent — assumptions (especially the absence of economies of large scale in addition to the absence of externalities), the converse is true. That is, every Pareto-optimal state of affairs can be reached through some competitive market equilibrium corresponding to some initial distribution of 'endowments' or resources owned.

The latter result — the 'converse theorem' — has been thought to be a great result in favour of the market mechanism, and so in some ways it is. If Pareto optimality is taken to be a necessary even though not a sufficient condition for overall optimality, then the fact that every Pareto-optimal outcome can be reached through the market mechanism does imply that — given the right conditions — the market mechanism can be used to reach even the very best social state.

However, three notes of caution should be introduced here. The first is the obvious one that the assumptions (such as no externality and no economy of large scale) are terribly demanding and will be often violated.

Second, while the 'converse theorem' is a tribute to the market mechanism, it is not a tribute to the invisible hand, that is to the market unassisted by political intervention. The initial distribution of resources has to be got right, and this, of course, does involve a political process, indeed — quite possibly — a totally revolutionary one requiring a thorough redistribution of the ownership of means of production, depending on the particular Pareto-optimal outcome that is identified as socially best. The contrast between capitalism and socialism is not the same as between market and non-market allocation. Indeed, many of the main results in the theory of resource allocation involving the market mechanism were first investigated and established by economists looking for socialist allocation procedures — Oscar Lange and Abba Lerner being two of the greatest of this class.

Third, while the result in question is a tribute to the market mechanism, it suggests the need to go beyond the market mechanism to get the information that would be needed to decide how best to distribute the resources initially. Under the market mechanism, given the right initial distribution and right prices, people may have the incentive to take the right decisions about production, consumption, and so on. But they do not have a similar incentive to reveal information about themselves that makes decisions regarding the initial distribution of resources possible. Disclosures about productive abilities, tastes, and so on can go against one's own interests in the determination of the initial distribution of resources, for example confession of higher ability or lower needs may have the effect of one's getting a lower share of non-labour resources in the initial split-up. There have been some suggestions about how to deal with this problem, but none really promises easy success.

Thus, the 'converse theorem' may, in fact, turn out to be of rather less practical interest than the first theorem, which simply asserts that under the specified conditions, no matter what initial distribution of resources we begin from, the outcome will be Pareto-optimal. Of course, as already mentioned, even in getting this result there are formidable difficulties since the assumptions needed are by no means easily fulfilled.

In discussing this question — the relevance of the first theorem — it is also worth bearing in mind that while Pareto optimality is some achievement, it is not in itself a grand prize. All that Pareto optimality implies is that there is no other feasible alternative that is better for everyone without exception, or better for some and no worse for anyone. A state in which some people are starving and suffering from acute deprivation while others are tasting the good life can still be Pareto optimal if the poor cannot be made better off without cutting into the pleasures of the rich — no matter by how small an amount. Pareto optimality is faint praise indeed.

In most economic problems the interests of the different people involved are partly congruent, partly conflicting. The market mechanism on its own confines its attention only to issues of congruence, leaving the interest conflicts unaddressed. It could, of course, turn out that the process of meeting the congruence interests itself might have the effect of reducing disparities and inequalities. For example, it has been argued that market-based economic growth of the type seen in the newly industrialized economies such as South Korea, Hong Kong, Taiwan and Singapore tends to be particularly beneficial to the poor — the potentially unwaged and unemployed. I shall presently have more to say on possible pitfalls in reading the experiences of these newly industrializing countries, but I do not doubt that there must be many examples all over the world in which the market-based pursuit of congruent interests has also reduced disparities. But there are also many examples in which precisely the opposite has happened. To take just one set of cases, there is strong evidence that the poor have shared relatively little in the fast economic growth in Latin America, and the congruent interests have been pursued in a way that has made the conflicts sharper and more violent.

Embedded in most problems of congruence is a problem of conflict, since the congruent interests can be pursued in many different ways with very different divisions of joint benefits. Both you and I may benefit from having some deal rather than none, and each may prefer having either of the deals, A and B, to no deal at all, but A may be better than B for you and B better than A for me. In the choice of *either* deal over *none*, our interests are congruent. In the choice *between* deals, they conflict. The situation in game-theoretic terms is one that J.F. Nash, the mathematician, has called a 'bargaining problem'.[8]

The market mechanism, with each person pursuing his self-interest, is geared to making sure that the congruent interests are exploited, but it does not offer a mechanism for harmonious or fair resolution of the problem of conflict that is inoperably embedded in the congruent exercise. The 'presumed harmony' referred to in the questionnaire discussed earlier, stands for, at best, a half-truth. The market division of benefits tends to reflect, roughly speaking, the economic 'power balance' of different individuals and groups — an idea that has been formalized in terms of the concept of the 'core'.[9]

Positional goods and public interest

One of the remarkable achievements of Fred Hirsch's analysis of 'social limits to growth' is the weaving together of the different types of failure that the market mechanism produces and to get from it an understanding of the malaise and the preoccupations of modern Western society. I shall not try to summarize that analysis, but I will comment on two particular points of immediate relevance to my discussion. Hirsch's concept of 'positional goods' helps us to understand why the elements of conflict have tended to acquire a new importance in the modern world. Many sources of enjoyment depend on the relative position of a person *vis-à-vis* others, for example, a person holding an eminent position in a job hierarchy, or — to take a different type of example — having access to an uncrowded beach. It is not possible to increase the supply of these positional goods, and one's ability to enjoy these goods depends on being ahead of others.

The increasing importance of positional goods has two important — and rather distinct — aspects. First, in case of any given positional good, there is no congruence of interest, since the total supply is fixed. In 'positional competition', as Hirsch explains, 'what winners win, losers lose'.[10] There is little scope for the market to enhance 'efficiency' through expanding the availability of positional goods.

However, this should not be taken to imply that the market cannot improve the well-being of all individuals in positional exchange, if exchange of different positional goods were possible. Indeed, the standard model of 'general equilibrium of exchange' also has the feature of having fixed total supply of goods. One positional good can be fruitfully exchanged for another *if* such exchanges were possible. This is where the second feature comes in. Most positional goods are not marketed and many of them are non-marketable. Thus the scope for mutually beneficial exchange of positional goods among the individuals happens to be severely limited. These two features together make the conflict elements dominate in the allocation of many of the positional goods, and make the congruent elements rather rare and difficult to exploit through the market mechanism.

Hirsch has pointed out that with material progress the pressure on positional goods has increased sharply. The fixity of total supply has made positional goods relatively scarce as the supplies of other goods have expanded. This has had the effect of making the market mechanism that much less adequate for the modern society.

Another force in the direction of making markets less adequate is the increasing importance of public goods — goods for which one person's consumption does not conflict with that of another. You and I may both benefit from a clean city centre, or a better television programme, without interfering with each other's consumption. Public goods involve strong congruence of interests, and as such it might be thought that the market mechanism should be able to deal with it very well. But in fact it cannot, since the market operates by insisting on a price to be paid for *possessing* a good, whereas in the case of public goods like enjoying a clean city centre or a good TV programme, such a pricing arrangement is not easy to devise. The market is good at taking care of issues of congruence of a special type only. It cannot handle well issues of conflict (including that involved in positional goods); nor issues of congruence in which the good in question is not individually possessed (as in the case of public goods).

The failure of the market mechanism based on the profit motive to deal with public goods is a specific example of its failure to deal with interdependences that work outside the price system. These problems have received a great deal of attention in the literature and the underlying analytical issues have been illustrated by games such as the Prisoner's Dilemma. There are various different ways of responding to this type of difficulty. One way is to use state intervention and the public sector.

Indeed, the enormous growth of the public sector in the recent years has not a little to do with this issue. Hirsch analyses this trend, but goes on to discuss another route, to wit, changing the behaviour norms, including the eschewal of the profit motive.[11]

Motives and outcomes

The rationale of Hirsch's suggestion regarding behavioural reorientation lies in the argument that self-interested behaviour may be collectively self-defeating. The Prisoner's Dilemma illustrates the problem very clearly.[12] Given the actions of others, it is in the interest of everyone to pursue self-interest directly, and each has a dominant strategy. But, for everyone it would have been better if they all had pursued some other, not directly self-interest-orientated, strategy. I shall have more to say on this presently, but before that a more elementary type of failure is worth discussing.

It is possible for the active pursuit of self-interest to be not only collectively self-defeating but also individually self-defeating. Even without any interpersonal interdependence of the kind referred to earlier, aiming directly at self-interest may be bad for achieving it.

Henry Sidgwick – that great utilitarian philosopher and economist — has pointed out that trying actively to maximize personal happiness may have the effect of producing a disposition that makes happiness difficult to achieve. Hayek's 'results of human action but not of human design' takes, incidentally, a rather serious form here. The question of choosing between dispositions has figured importantly in the writings of such philosophers as Richard Hare, Robert Adams and Jon Elster. Having a roving eye for the quick 'utile' might well be disastrous for achieving happiness.

The cultivation of achievement-orientated motivation in the modern society can indeed produce psychological and social barriers to personal happiness. Motivational uptightness can be a serious impediment to enjoying life. The activist who, to vary a famous presidential description, can chew gum *only when* he is crossing the street, certainly has some problems. So has the person who relentlessly pursues positional success.

The agony of the maximizer may be less known to the economist than to the novelist, but it is no less important for that reason. Indeed, the neglect of serious psychological issues in traditional economics is truly remarkable, and it is only recently that this lacuna has begun to get some response in the writings of — in addition to Fred Hirsch — Albert Hirschman, Janos Kornai, Tibor Scitovsky, Harvey Leibenstein, Thomas Schelling, George Akerlof and William Dickens, and others.[13]

Procedural assessment

I have so far been proceeding on the implicit understanding that the market mechanism has to be assessed in terms of its results. That implicit assumption has been shared by economists of very different schools of thought — from Milton Friedman to John Kenneth Galbraith. The differences between the schools on this issue have centred on the question as to what results the profit motive and the market mechanism do, in fact, have. There is, however, a well-developed philosophical approach in social theory arguing against end-state judgements. For example, Robert Nozick, in his influential and important book, *Anarchy, State and Utopia*,[14] has argued in favour of downgrading consequence-based evaluation into a minor secondary position compared with the imperative of the right procedural rules. Nozick has seen a collection of rights, including those of ownership and transfer, as central. Individuals have these rights and 'there are things no person or group may do to them'. Since the rights of ownership and transfer including exchange, markets are, in this view, justified by antecedent rights rather than by consequent outcomes. Nozick points to (what he calls) 'invisible-hand explanations' of the emergence of social institutions (such as markets), citing Adam Smith,[15] but there is no assessment of such institutions in terms of the goodness of interest-fulfilling outcomes. If this view is accepted, then the focus of traditional discussion of the merits and demerits of the market is quite misplaced, since the right to exchange exists no matter what the consequences of such market operations happen to be. The focus is on 'entitlements', not on results.

This approach involves a major philosophical departure and, *inter alia*, it rejects seeing markets in the way economists have typically done, that is in terms of what markets do to people's interests (rather than how people's rights require markets). I believe these procedural issues deserve a great deal more attention than economists have been inclined to give them, and Nozick's analysis represents just one example of non-consequentialist moral reasoning which is potentially of much relevance to welfare economics.[16] While I shall not pursue this complex philosophical question here, which I have tried to do elsewhere,[17] I should make two remarks on this approach specifically related to the main enquiry.

First, the justification of markets in terms of rights of ownership and transfer is independent of the exact nature of human motivation in a way that a consequence-based assessment of markets cannot be. What guides people in undertaking exchange in the market matters not at all in justifying the markets, since it is their privilege to be guided by whatever they like irrespective of consequences. Thus, while the Nozickian approach is pro-market, it need not be pro-profit-motive in any sense. People are free to pursue profits if they so choose, but they need not, and Nozick gives some good reasons as to why they may choose not to.[18]

Second, any consequence-independent justification suffers from the possibility that the consequences may be so disastrous that the entire approach may look altogether implausible. Nozick does not deal with this issue at all adequately, and states that 'the question of whether these side constraints reflecting rights are absolute, or whether they may be violated in order to avoid catastrophic moral horror, and if the latter, what the resulting structure might look like, is one I hope largely to avoid'.[19] But this is a serious issue to leave open, since permitting violation of allegedly consequence-independent rights is the thin end of the wedge. Once consequence-based arguments are accepted as relevant, then it is not clear what obvious stopping place there is for a theory that was set up on a purely procedural approach.

Consequences, disasters and achievements.

Terrible consequences emerging from the exercise of rights in market situations are not only imaginable in theory, they are also observable in the real world. Elsewhere[20] I have presented evidence to indicate that many famines — even very big ones — have taken place in the recent past with no overall decline of food availability, and millions have died because of being deprived of food in terms of market command, reflecting sharp failures of entitlement. There is something deeply implausible about asserting that justification of rules of ownership, exchange and market operations can be really consequence-independent, and in this case unaffected by matters of life and death.

It is, of course, true that such terrible consequences have not occurred in the richer market-based economies of the West. People do not go begging for food in the countries that are now called, merciless to geography, the North. But this is not the result of any guarantee that the market or profit maximization has provided, but rather due to the social security that the state has offered. With the magnitude of unemployment being what it is today in Western Europe or North America, the 'entitlements' of many millions of people in the moral system based on ownership have amounted to next to nothing. The reason why these countries have not been visited by disaster is precisely the existence of systematic transfers through the state of the kind that the moral entitlement theory does so much to reject.

I should not, however, concentrate my attention only on the failures of the market system and must look also at the achievements. Indeed, the last few decades have also been seen as years of great cheer for the market mechanism. Until fairly recently the richer market economies have grown very fast in economic terms. While over the last two decades the growth rate of gross national product per capita in the 'industrial market economies' (3.6 per cent over 1960–80), has been a little lower than that of 'non-market industrial economies', that is the richer communist countries (4.2 per cent),[21] the world record of fast growth among all the richer countries — market and non-market — is held by Japan (7.1 per cent). Also, the high growth rate of several 'non-market economies' has been combined with remarkable shortages in specific goods, including food.

As far as the poorer economies are concerned, if we concentrate attention on countries outside Europe and North America, the highest growth performers over the period 1960–80 have been Singapore (7.5 per cent), South Korea (7.0 per cent), and Hong Kong (6.8 per cent).[22] These are, of course, all economies with private ownership and markets. The fact that these countries have combined fast economic growth with no noticeable worsening of the relative distribution of incomes has received, with justice, much admiration and many eulogies. The literature on the theory of economic development is beginning to reflect appreciation of these performances. One of the most distinguished examples of this type of analysis can be found in Ian Little's new book on *Economic Development*.[23] The 'old guards' at that side of the fence, such as Peter Bauer who wrote such a lonely — but excellent — book called *Dissent on Development*,[24] can rejoice at this trend, and Bauer can with justified pride write a new book reflecting the changing professional opinion and call it, perhaps, *Assent at Long Last on Development*.

There is, however, some difficulty in reading the experiences of the east Asian newly industrializing countries — countries that Ian Little calls by the delightful name 'baby tigers'.[25] Hong Kong and Singapore are essentially city economies, and if we look at growth rates of cities, there are others that compare with the performance of these baby tigers, which benefit from being babies at least in size. There are no great rural masses to drag them down. But South Korea is a fairly large country, and is no city state. The difficulty, however, in reading great significance into the performance of South Korea as a success story for the 'invisible hand' is the fact that the hands that reared South Korean growth were very visible indeed. The government played a major part in fostering economic growth in South Korea, and, as has been argued, 'no state outside the socialist bloc ever came anywhere near this measure of control over the economy's investible resources'.[26] Indeed, adding government savings to deposits in nationalized banks, the South Korean government had control over two-thirds of the investment resources in the country in the period of its rapid acceleration of growth. This governmental power was firmly used to guide investment in chosen directions through differential interest rates and credit availabilities. I have discussed this question in some detail elsewhere.[27] Even Korean export expansion was founded on building an industrial base through severe import controls before export promotion was promoted, and even now the import of many items is restricted or prohibited. The economic expansion was directly orchestrated by an activist central government.

In fact it is remarkable that if we look at the sizeable developing countries, the fast-growing and otherwise high-performing countries have all had governments that have been directly and actively involved in the planning of economic and social performance. I do not mean that they have powerful governments — that is certainly the case but that is true of almost all developing countries anyway. I mean that the governments have been involved with economic planning and with deliberate and ambitious public action. The types of planning used have varied between, say, China, Sri Lanka, South Korea and Yugoslavia, but their respective successes are directly linked to deliberation and design, rather than being just the results of uncoordinated profit-seeking or atomistic pursuit of self-interest. I have discussed these issues elsewhere,[28] and will not pursue them further here.

Motives and behaviour

The issue of public action is, however, rather different from that of the best orientation of individual behaviour. In this respect, the ambitious Chinese attempt at replacing the profit motive and self-seeking by non-incentive systems seems to have been acknowledged as a failure. Certainly, the extent of cultural reorientation that was called for required such a drastic revision of human motivation that it would have been totally remarkable if it had been an easy success.

But it would be a mistake to think that the alternatives to the profit motive must, of necessity, take such a drastic form. In our day-to-day actions there is much scope for departing from self-seeking in a less grand way. There is, in fact, very little doubt that neither the family as a social unit nor the firm as an economic unit can really operate entirely on the basis of individual self-seeking. Norms of behaviour depart from that not only *vis-à-vis* other members of the family but in terms of loyalty to colleagues and to the firm.

To some extent this has been observed in all types of economy, but the scope for such non-profit behaviour also varies greatly between countries. It has been argued with much force and plausibility that the success of the Japanese economy owes not a little to what Michio Morishima has recently called 'the Japanese ethos'.[29] which clearly has deep historical roots. The extent of loyalty, co-operation, sense of duty, and public spirit that is observed in Japanese factories is evidently in sharp contrast with what can be found in, say, Britain.

There is little doubt that the Japanese attitude to private gain and public duty differs greatly from that in other rich, industrial countries. Much has been written on that contrast. The differences in social psychology play a major part not only in economic performance but also in such other communal matters as the lower crime rate, much less frequent litigation (indeed, far fewer lawyers per unit of population), and so on. If the invisible hand does a great deal of visible good in Japan, the hand does not seem to work through the relentless pursuit of self-interest.

In fact, when one considers how production takes place in a modern industrial establishment, it is quite incredible to think that being actively self-interested can be such a virtue. Success in production depends greatly on team work, and while that interdependent picture provides incentive for a group, it is not an incentive that can be effectively translated into rewards and punishments related to individual work and performance.

Milton Friedman has argued that 'the process of "natural selection" . . . helps to validate the hypothesis' of profit maximization.[30] The profit-maximizing firms survive and do better. This process may indeed work *if* deliberate attempts at profit maximization are likely to produce more actual profits and more expansion. However, when it comes to individual workers, the argument does not translate at all. Indeed, in so far as workers with better team spirit do better than self-interest-maximizing workers, one might expect the argument to favour the development of team spirit rather than of maximization of individual interests or profits. Morishima's historical account of the emergence of the Japanese ethos may be supplemented by an argument for sustenance through better survival.

Fred Hirsch's analysis of the need to reorientate behaviour norms is very relevant here. His argument is this:

where individual preferences can be satisfied in sum only or most efficiently through collective action, privately directed behaviour may lose its inherent advantages over collectively oriented behaviour *even as a means to satisfying individual preferences themselves*, however, self-interested. It follows that the best result may be attained by steering or guiding certain motives of individual behaviour into social rather than individual orientation, though still on the basis of privately directed preferences. This requires not a change in human nature, 'merely' a change in human convention or instinct or attitude of the same order as the shifts in social conventions or moral standards that have gone along with major changes in economic conditions in the past.[31]

In understanding this proposed solution, it is important to see that Hirsch is not arguing for a change of what people actually would like to achieve. It is not an argument for changing one's goals, which of course will be a defeatist solution to the problem at hand (no matter how desirable for other reasons). The argument is a strategic one for better achieving the given self-interested objectives. Self-interest-based objectives are achieved better for the group as a whole by the individuals *behaving* differently, *as if* they are maximizing some other objectives.[32] The so-called 'Japanese ethos' can be just the ethos of behaviour and not necessarily of having different ultimate objectives.

Roles, information and self-interest

At this stage of the discussion, a different type of difficulty altogether may be considered. Surely the Adam Smithian argument about the merits of self-interested behaviour in the context of exchange builds on the twin facts that (1) such behaviour gives everyone the *role* of protecting and pursuing his or her own interests, and (2) the interests of each person are best *known* by the person himself or herself. While such behaviour does not resolve conflicts, nor take care of pursuing congruent interests in the presence of interdependences of the kind specified, it does help in the fulfilment of many congruent interests. Are we not in danger of losing even the limited virtues of self-interest maximization (related to role division and informational efficiency) if the motivational parameters change?

More other-regarding behaviour, unless it is specially symmetrical, can certainly lead to very unequal coverage of different people's interests. An assumption of 'symmetric goodwill' will be quite exacting.[33] It can, however, be pointed out that the market mechanism, even with self-interested behaviour, does not deal with issues of equity at all satisfactorily, and indeed, as already discussed, does not properly address the question of interest conflicts at all. Non-symmetric goodwill might introduce another element of asymmetry in the pursuit of different people's interests, but it would not necessarily make the overall situation less just or more inequitable. Indeed, we can say very little in general about how the equity side of the picture will change with a motivational shift from self-interested behaviour, since so little can be said generally about equity under self-interest behaviour.

The change on the informational issue is, however, easier to see and assess. Even if I pursue your interests with the same vigour as you would, and you pursue my interests in the same breathless way as I would, we may do worse jobs of these functions than if we were to look after our own interests themselves. This recognition does nothing to wash away the problems of interdependence identified by Fred Hirsch and others and the failure of self-interest-based behaviour to deal with those problems. But superimposed on those problems are also some problems of informed pursuit of different people's respective interests, and replacing self-interested behaviour by other-regarding behaviour may punch a new hole as it plugs an old one.

It is interesting that there has been so little discussion of the impact of motivational change on the result of market equilibrium. There are, of course, some interesting and analytically important results about how special types of altruism might preserve some of the links between Pareto optimality and competitive equilibria.[34] But these results have been derived in quite a limited format, using strong assumptions, and they are in particular based on ignoring the force of the informational problem.

Some have seen relatively little difficulty in the market system being able to accommodate a great variety of motivational assumptions without losing its virtues. For example, in his lucid and illuminating report on the survey of the views of British economists (discussed earlier), Samuel Brittan refuses to be impressed by the assumption of the pursuit of self-interest in guaranteeing the achievements of the market. He remarks: 'the success of a competitive free enterprise economy, working under the right environmental policies, depends on people pursuing *self-chosen* interests, which can be altruistic, aesthetic or anything else.[35] This is indeed so up to a point, in the sense that it may be possible to replace the achievement of, say, Pareto optimality by achieving a corresponding condition of non-improvability in terms of the different people's goals — whatever they are — rather than their self-interest or utilities.

On the other hand, other-regarding goals raise problems of consistency and coherence in a way that independent self-interests of different people do not. We can both try to do good to each other and end up failing to serve either person's interests. One has only to recollect O. Henry's story 'The Gift of the Magi' to see how the pursuit of altruism can lead to frustration.

Robin Matthews[36] has discussed lucidly how the information-revealing role of the pursuit of self-interest may be lost if people do behave according to some moral norms, for example, those given by act utilitarianism. The person who knows an individual best is the individual himself or herself, and this signalling function may well be quite lost if rather than acting on the basis of personal self-interest one pursues other goals. Doing good is not an easy matter with informational deficiency. (I remember the embarrassment of a friend who, staying as the guest of a family in Bombay, decided to make herself useful and spent the afternoon polishing up a small dirty-looking metal statue she found in the living room to discover later that she had made a thirteenth century icon look sparklingly modern.)

There are, in fact, the horns of a dilemma here. If individuals pursue goals other than the pursuit of self-interest, they can mess up the market mechanism informationally and also produce problems of consistency and coherence. On the other hand, if they do act selfishly, then they prevent the market from achieving efficiency in the presence of interdependences, not to mention other goals such as addressing problems of conflict.

What has to be recognized clearly is the unreality — and over-ambitiousness — of the neat, harmonious picture of social good coming from coherent and independent choices of individuals — a picture that has so deeply influenced economics. That account misses the real world by many miles. It is not easy — perhaps impossible — to replace that old model of success based on self-interested individuals, by another one with the same degree of ambition, and to get with equal ease a similarly neat picture of social good coming from the individual pursuit of some other simple motivation.

Some general conclusions

First, the central economic problem can be seen as that of fulfilling congruent interests of different people, along with dealing with conflicts of interest fairly. The 'invisible hand' in the form of the market mechanism is geared to the congruence exercise, with the conflict problem unaddressed and essentially left to the equilibrium of relative powers and muscles (formalized in the notion of the 'core'). Despite claims to the contrary, the market and the profit motive cannot guarantee bringing about a 'harmony' of interests.

Second, the profit motive is, of course, a very powerful force and it can certainly do wonders. Its success is partly due to the fact that quite often the interdependences underlying congruent interests can be captured within the market mechanism. The market mechanism succeeds, under these circumstances, because of the *fulfilment* of non-conflicting individual designs, and it is quite misleading to see this achievement as 'a result of human action but not of human design'.

Third, the conflict problem is, obviously, not amenable to solution in this way, and this failure can take a serious, even disastrous, form. Even the congruence problem may be insoluble through the market and profit motive, if the congruence in the market mechanism with a price tag attached to each benefit and cost. The market is best at dealing with only one kind of congruence of interests.

Fourth, purely procedural justifications of the market independently of consequences — while interesting and challenging — ultimately lack plausibility. They do not, incidentally, do anything to support the profit motive.

Fifth, the profit motive and self-interest-based action can be self-defeating. Specialist maximizers can produce very general failures. There is the problem of being collectively self-defeating because of interdependences that elude the market, and these are of increasing importance, as Fred Hirsch has argued. There is, in addition, the problem of being individually self-defeating because of psychological conflicts between motivation and realization.

Sixth, while the problem of being individually self-defeating raises deep psychological issues, that of being collectively self-defeating raises questions of state action and co-operative efforts. It also points towards the case for behaviour modification. It is in that context important, as Hirsch has emphasized, to examine the possibility of behaviour norms that break away from the pursuit of self-interest by individuals the better to achieve the fulfilment of those very interests. There is a clear link between this type of theory and the observed success of some economies, most importantly in Japan.

Seventh, departures from self-interest maximization help in some respects but also hinder in other ways. Self-interest maximization serves to channel information into the market procedures; each pursuing the interests of others can, in many contexts, be informationally defective. Indeed, it is not easy to see that some rule of behaviour of the same type of generality as the pursuit of self-interest can, in fact, avoid both the Scylla of interdependence failures and the Charybdis of informational deficiency.

What goes wrong with the traditional model of the invisible hand is not just the limitation of relying exclusively on self-interest, but the stunning ambitiousness of trying to guarantee social efficiency — not to mention social optimality — on the basis of *independent* pursuit by individuals of some general objective (such as profits). This negative recognition, however, does nothing to undermine the importance of studying alternative behaviour norms and examining their consequences. Behaviour norms have to be assessed in the light of comparative achievements rather than just in terms of the attainment or not of efficiency or optimality. The effectiveness of non-profit behaviour is important in that less ambitious but more practical context.

Finally, I should point out that I have not had the opportunity to go into a fundamental question which Adam Smith touched on and thought to be important. Should motivation be determined entirely by usefulness, or are there other important values to consider? Should the profit motive be recommended to all if it has proved impeccably useful? Should the 'Japanese ethos' be cultivated by all if it is really as useful as it seems to be? Adam Smith would have disputed that usefulness is all that is involved. Indeed, he did think that to praise a person for his useful qualities is to confuse him or her with something like a piece of furniture or a building:

it seems possible that the approbation of virtue should be a sentiment of the same kind with that by which we approve of a convenient or well-contrived building, or that we should have no other reason for praising a man than that for which we commend a chest of drawers.[37]

While I have concentrated on assessing motivations in terms of their usefulness, I would not deny that Adam Smith is right and this cannot provide a full view of that important question. Even as economists we cannot altogether escape this deeper valuational issue. The subject is dismal enough as it is.

Notes

1. F.A. Hayek, *Studies in Philosophy, Politics and Economics*, Chicago, 1967, pp. 96–105.
2. Ibid., pp. 99–100.
3. Samuel Brittan, *Is There an Economic Consensus? An Attitude Survey*, London, 1973.
4. J. Kearl, C. Pope, G. Whiting and L. Wimmer, 'A Confusion of Economists?', *American Economic Review Proceedings*, vol. 69, 1979.
5. F. Hahn, 'Reflections on the Invisible Hand', *Lloyds Bank Review*, no. 144, April 1982; reprinted in this volume.
6. F. Hirsch, *The Social Limits to Growth*, London, 1977.
7. Adam Smith, *An Inquiry into the Nature and Causes of the Wealth of Nations* (1776), London, 1910, Book I, Chapter II, vol. 1, p. 13.
8. J.F. Nash, 'The Bargaining Problem', *Econometrica*, vol. 18, 1950.
9. See K.J. Arrow and F. Hahn, *General Competitive Analysis*, San Francisco, 1971.
10. Hirsch, *The Social Limits to Growth*, p. 52.
11. Ibid., p. 146.
12. See A. Sen, 'Behaviour and the Concept of Preference', *Economica*, vol. 40, 1973, reprinted in A. Sen, *Choice, Welfare and Measurement*, Oxford, 1982; and Derek Parfit, 'Prudence Morality, and the Prisoner's Dilemma', *Proceedings of the British Academy for 1979*, London, 1981.
13. A.O. Hirschman, *Exit, Voice and Loyalty*, Cambridge, MA, 1970; A. O. Hirschman, *Shifting Involvements: Private and Public Action*, Princeton, NJ, 1982; J. Kornai, *Anti-Equilibrium*, Amsterdam, 1971; T., Scitovsky, *The Joyless Economy*, Oxford, 1976; Harvey Leibenstein, *Beyond Economic Man: A New Foundation for Microeconomics*, Cambridge MA, 1976; Thomas Schelling, *Micromotives and Macrobehaviour*, New York, 1978; George Akerlof and William T. Dickens, 'The Economic Consequences of Cognitive Dissonance', *American Economic Review*, vol. 72, 1982. Howard Margolis, *Selfishness, Altruism and Rationality*, Cambridge, 1982. See also the important critique of Robert Solow in his AEA Presidential Address, 'On Theories of Unemployment', *American Economic Review*, vol. 70, 1980. For some sceptical notes by one of the founders, see John Hicks, 'The Measurement of Real Income', *Oxford Economic Papers*, vol. 10, 1958, reprinted in his *Wealth and Welfare*, Oxford, 1981, pp. 148–50.
14. R. Nozick, *Anarchy, State and Utopia*, New York, 1974.
15. Smith, *Wealth of Nations*, p. 18.
16. See A. Sen and B. Williams (eds) *Utilitarianism and Beyond*, Cambridge, 1982.
17. Especially in A. Sen, 'Rights and Agency', *Philosophy and Public Affairs*, vol. 11, 1982; and A. Sen, 'Liberty and Social Choice', *Journal of Philosophy*, vol. 80, 1983.
18. Nozick, *Anarchy, State and Utopia*, Chapter 8.

19. Ibid., p. 30.
20. A. Sen, *Poverty and Famines: An Essay on Entitlement and Deprivation*, Oxford, 1981.
21. *World Development Report*, Washington DC, 1982, Table 1.
22. Ibid.
23. I.M.D. Little, *Economic Development: Theory, Policy, and International Relations*, New York, 1982.
24. P.T. Bauer, *Dissent on Development*, London, 1971.
25. Little, *Economic Development*, p. 262.
26. M.K. Datta-Chaudhuri, 'Industrialization and Foreign Trade: An Analysis Based on the Development Experience of the Republic of Korea and the Philippines', ILO Working Paper WP II-4, Asian Employment Programme, ARTEP, ILO, Bangkok, 1979.
27. A. Sen, 'Public Action and the Quality of Life in Developing Countries', *Oxford Bulletin of Economics and Statistics*, vol. 43, 1981.
28. A. Sen, 'Development: Which Way Now?' Presidential Address, Development Studies Association, given in Dublin, September 1982.
29. Michio Morishima, *Why has Japan 'Succeeded'? Western Technology and Japanese Ethos*, Cambridge, 1982.
30. Milton Friedman, *Essays in Positive Economics*, Chicago, 1953, p. 22.
31. Hirsch, *Social Limits to Growth*, p. 146.
32. See A. Sen, *On Economic Inequality*, Oxford, 1973; and A. Sen, 'Choice, Orderings and Morality', in S Körner, ed. *Practical Reason*, Oxford, 1974, reprinted in Sen, *Choice, Welfare and Measurement*. See also George Akerlof, 'Loyalty Filters', mimeo, Institute of Business and Economic Research, University of California, Berkeley, 1982.
33. CF. A. Sen, 'Labour Allocation in a Cooperative Enterprise', *Review of Economic Studies*, vol. 33, 1966; David Collard, *Altruism and Economy*, Oxford, 1978.
34. See S.G. Winter, Jr, 'A Simple Remark on the Second Optimality Theorem of Welfare Economics', *Journal of Economic Theory*, vol. 1, 1969; G.C. Archibald and D. Donaldson, 'Non-Paternalism and Basic Theorems of Welfare Economics', *Canadian Journal of Economics*, vol. 9, 1976; Collard, *Altruism and Economy*.
35. *Is There an Economic Consensus?*, p. 53. See also R. Sugden, 'On the Economics of Philanthropy', *Economic Journal*, vol. 92, 1982; A.J. Oswald, 'An Approach to the Economics of Unselfishness', mimeo, St John's College, Oxford, 1982.
36. R.C.O. Matthews, 'Morality, Competition and Efficiency', *Manchester School*, 1981.
37. A. Smith, *The Theory of Moral Sentiments*, IV 24, p. 188. The immediate provocation for Smith's remark is Hume's analysis of virtue in terms of 'utility' (in the sense of usefulness).

8 On the efficiency of the financial system
James Tobin

The United States, as befits the major capitalist economy of the world, has the largest, most elaborate, most sophisticated financial industry in the world. New York is rivalled only by London, which thanks to long-standing international connections and experience, maintains a financial role disproportionate to Britain's declining position in world trade and production. Moreover, finance is one of the United States' rapid growth sectors.

Just the other day, the *New York Times* listed 46 business executives whose 1983 compensation (salary and bonus, exclusive of realizations of previously acquired stock options) exceeded 1 million dollars. What struck me was that 16 members of this elite were officers of financial companies.[1] No wonder, then, that finance is the favourite destination of the undergraduates I teach at Yale, and that 40 per cent of 1983 graduates of our School of Organization and Management took jobs in finance.[2] Their starting salaries are four times the poverty threshold for four-person families. All university educators know that finance is engaging a large and growing proportion of the most able young men and women in the country. Later in this lecture I shall present further information on the economic size of our financial industries.

Fred Hirsch, gifted economist and social critic, took all institutions, private as well as public, to be fair game for analysis and evaluation. He was not willing to assume on faith or principle that 'markets' work for the best, or to blame distortions solely on government interventions and regulations. Nor did he have illusions that legislatures and bureaucracies work for the best. In the same spirit I decided to use this lecture to voice some sceptical views of the efficiency of our vast system of financial markets and institutions. These views run against current tides — not only the general enthusiasm for deregulation and unfettered competition but my profession's intellectual admiration for the efficiency of financial markets.

James Tobin is Emeritus Professor of Economics at Yale University, and won the Nobel Prize in Economic Science in 1981. This article is a revised version of the Fred Hirsch Memorial Lecture given in New York on 15 May 1984. It first appeared in *Lloyds Bank Review*, no. 153, July 1984.

Finance theory itself is a burgeoning activity in academia, occupying more and more faculty slots, student credit hours, journal pages, and computer printouts, both in management schools and in economics departments. And as the newspapers have been reporting, finance academics are finding their way to the street.[3]

Efficiency

Efficiency has several different meanings. First, a market is 'efficient' if it is on average impossible to gain from trading on the basis of generally available public information. In efficient markets only insiders can make money, consistently anyway. Whatever you and I know the market has already 'discounted'. The revealing standard anecdote goes like this: Finance professor is walking on campus with his research assistant, who says, 'Professor, I see a twenty dollar bill on the sidewalk. Should I pick it up?' 'No, of course not, if it were really there, it would already have been picked up.' Efficiency in this meaning I call *information-arbitrage* efficiency.

A second and deeper meaning is the following: a market in a financial asset is efficient if its valuations reflect accurately the future payments to which the asset gives title — to use currently fashionable jargon, if the price of the asset is based on 'rational expectations' of those payments. I call this concept *fundamental-valuation* efficiency.

Third, a system of financial markets is efficient if it enables economic agents to ensure for themselves deliveries of goods and services in all future contingencies, either by surrendering some of their own resources now or by contracting to deliver them in specified future contingencies. Contracts for specified goods in specified 'states of nature' are called in economic theory *Arrow–Debreu contracts*. Kenneth Arrow and Gerard Debreu showed rigorously that a complete set of competitive markets of this kind is necessary and, given some other conditions, sufficient to guarantee the existence of an equilibrium with the optimal properties intuitively perceived by Adam Smith and succeeding generations of free market theorists.[4] I call efficiency in this Arrow–Debreu sense *full-insurance* efficiency.

The fourth concept relates more concretely to the economic functions of the financial industries. They do not provide services directly useful to producers or to consumers. That sentence is an overstatement, because some people enjoy gambling *per se*, and prefer the securities market to casinos and race tracks. But the resources devoted to financial services are generally justified on other grounds. These include: the pooling of risks and their allocation to those most able and willing to bear them, a generalized insurance function in the Arrow–Debreu spirit just discussed; the facilitation of transactions by providing mechanisms and networks of payments; the mobilization of saving for investments in physical and human capital, domestic and foreign, private and public, and the allocation of savings to their more socially productive uses. I call efficiency in these respects *functional* efficiency.

Before discussing the American financial system in terms of these four criteria of efficiency, I want to point out that the services of the system do not come cheap. An immense volume of activity takes place, and considerable resources are devoted to it. Let me remind you of some of the relevant magnitudes.

The Department of Commerce categories Finance and Insurance generate 4½–5 per cent of GNP, account for 5½ per cent of employee compensation, and occupy about 5 per cent of the employed labour force. They account for 7½ per cent of after-tax corporate profits. About 3 per cent of personal consumption, as measured by the Commerce Department, is accounted for by financial services. These figures do not include the legal profession, which amounts to about 1 per cent of the economy, and a significant fraction of its business is financial in nature.[5]

The measures just reported do not tell the complete story. They cover only the value added by the labour and capital directly employed. If the inputs of goods and services purchased from other industries are included, Finance and Insurance use about 9 per cent of the GNP.[6]

Thirty billion shares of stock, valued at US$1,000 billion, changed hands in 1983. The turnover was 60 per cent of the outstanding shares. Thus the average holding period is about 19 months. Assuming conservatively that costs are 1½ per cent of dollar volume, traders paid $14 billion. In fact, the expenses and after-tax profits of New York Stock Exchange member forms were, in 1982, $22 billion, 3⅓ per cent of the value of transactions. The securities industry employed 232,000 persons, including 61,000 sales representatives, out of approximately 5,000 sales offices. The turnover of stocks in the United States is greater than in any other country. The closest competitors are Japan (35 per cent), West Germany (24 per cent), and Britain (16 per cent).

The American secondary market in bonds, in contrast to stocks is very inactive. Annual transactions of $7.2 billion on the New York Stock Exchange are less than 1 per cent of the par value or market value of the listed bonds. For another comparison, consider one-family homes. Annual sales, of which one-sixth are new homes, amount to 4½ per cent of the existing stock.[7]

Stocks and bonds are by no means the only instruments traded on organized markets. The pages of the *Wall Street Journal* report markets in options as follows: 4,000 contracts on 475 common stocks varying in date and striking price; 100 contracts on 15 stock indexes; 60 contracts on 5 foreign currencies, 11 contracts on 3 interest rates. There are also some 500 futures contracts traded, varying as to future date, covering 40 commodities, 5 foreign exchange rates, 10 interest rates or bond prices, and 6 stock indexes. There are even 100 'futures options' contracts. Transactions volumes in all these markets are substantial but difficult to measure in terms comparable to transactions in primary securities.

Our 15,000 commercial banks do business from 60,000 banking offices, one for every 3,800 persons. The operating expenses of commercial banks were $61 billion in 1982. Of these $10 billion were annualized 'occupancy expenses', $170,000 per office.[8] In addition, 4,250 savings institutions with 25,750 offices had operating expenses of $14 billion.[9]

Information-arbitrage efficiency

The long-standing judgement of almost all academics in economics and finance is yes, securities markets are efficient in this sense. The first study to indicate this result was by Alfred Cowles, the founder of the Cowles Commission, now the Cowles Foundation at Yale. An investment adviser himself, chastened by the stock market's gyrations from 1928 to 1933, he showed statistically that an investor would have done at least as well choosing stocks at random as following professional advice.[10] His conclusions have been confirmed many times in different ways. As a statistical matter actively managed portfolios, with allowance made for transaction costs, do not beat the market. Prices are a random walk in the sense that their correlations with past histories are too weak to be exploited profitably.[11] These findings contradict the claims of 'technical' analysis. They suggest, in general, that the mathematical expectation of return from resources used in active portfolio management is zero for the clients of brokers and investment advisers and for the owners of mutual funds.

Efficiency in information-based arbitrage does not come free. It requires resource inputs from abitrageurs, specialists, market-makers. Random walking does not, of course, mean that prices are unresponsive to new information. On the contrary, it means that they respond promptly and fully — and conceivably with little or no trading.

Fundamental-valuation efficiency

This brings me to the second kind of efficiency, the accuracy with which market valuations reflect fundamentals. Efficiency in this sense is by no means implied by the technical efficiency just discussed. There are good reasons to be sceptical.

The fundamentals for a stock are the expected future dividends or other payouts, or, what amounts in principle to the same thing, the expected future earnings. The stock's value is the present discounted value of either of these streams. Casual observation suggests that the market moves up and down much more than can be justified by changes in rationally formed expectations, or in the rates at which they are discounted. This suspicion has been rigorously verified by my colleague Robert Shiller.[12] Evidently market speculation multiplies severalfold the underlying fundamental variability of dividends and earnings.

Shiller has also demonstrated the analogous empirical proposition for the bond market.[13] The yield of a long-term bond is in principle a kind of average of the short-term interest rates expected to prevail in sequence from now to the bond's maturity. Bond prices fluctuate much more than the variability of short rates can justify. Stephen Golub and others have shown that foreign exchange rates are excessively volatile relative to fluctuations in trade balances.[14]

Equity prices have been a puzzle for the last decade, falling well below the replacement value of the underlying capital assets and the present value of the payouts those assets could be expected to earn.[15] Among the hypotheses advanced was one by Modigliani and Cohn, that the market was not allowing for inflation in the streams of earnings and dividends but was discounting real streams by interest rates containing substantial premiums for expected inflation.[16] The authors made a convincing statistical argument for such irrational downward bias, and corroborated it by quotations from professional market advisers displaying the misunderstanding. The Modigliani–Cohn thesis is controversial and is probably not the whole story. Whatever the sources of the chronic undervaluation, it is evidently nothing that arbitrage could or did correct.

Take-over mania, motivated by egregious undervaluations, is testimony to the failure of the market on this fundamental-valuation criterion of efficiency. A take-over mobilizes enough capital to jump the price of the target stock to levels much closer to the fundamental value of the underlying assets, for example, Gulf's oil reserves. Ordinary investors might have detected the same undervaluations, but could not expect to profit from them unless and until other ordinary investors agreed — or a take-over materialized. Take-overs serve a useful function if they bring prices closer to fundamental values. But the fact that markets fail to do so on their own is a serious indictment of their efficiency.

J.M. Keynes likened the stock market — and he referred particularly to the American market —

to those newspaper competitions in which the competitors have to pick out the six prettiest faces from a hundred photographs, the prize being awarded to the competitor whose choice most nearly corresponds to the average preferences of the competitors as a whole; so that each competitor has to pick, not those faces which he himself finds prettiest, but those which he thinks likeliest to catch the fancy of the other competitors, all of whom are looking at the problem from the same point of view . . . [We] have reached the third degree where we devote our intelligences to anticipating what average opinion expects the average opinion to be. And there are some, I believe, who practice the fourth, fifth, and higher degrees.[17]

Speculations on the speculations of other speculators who are doing the same thing — those are 'bubbles'. They dominate, of course, the pricing of assets with negligible fundamentals, zero or vague or non-transferable returns in consumption of production. Gold and collectables, for example, derive value almost wholly from guesses about the opinions of future speculators. But bubbles are also, as Keynes observed, phenomena of markets for equities, long-term bonds, foreign exchange, commodity futures, and real estate.

Keynes, himself an active and experienced market participant, despaired of 'investment based on genuine long-term expectation.' There is no clear evidence from experience, he said, 'that the investment policy which is socially advantageous coincides with that which is most profitable.' He noted that professionals who bet on long-term fundamentals, while everyone else is engaged in short-term attempts 'to guess better than the crowd how the crowd will behave', run greater risks. Not least of these is criticism for unconventional and rash investment behaviour. Keynes's views would be confirmed today if he observed how professional portfolio managers seek safety from criticism in short-run performances that match their competitors and market indices.

Keynes's pessimism on the long-term rationality of securities markets led him to the view that the liquidity these markets provide is a mixed blessing. 'The spectacle . . . has sometimes moved me towards the conclusion that to make the purchase of an investment permanent and indissoluble, like marriage (sic!), except by reason of death or other grave cause, might be a useful remedy . . .'. But he concluded that illiquidity would be the worse evil, because it would push savers towards hoarding of money. Today that disadvantage seems less serious than when Keynes was writing, during the Great Depression. Anyway, he advocated as a half-way measure a 'substantial . . . transfer tax . . . , with a view of mitigating the predominance of speculation over enterprise in the United States'. For similar reasons, I have advocated an international transfer tax on transactions across currencies.[18]

Full-insurance efficiency

My third concept is drawn from the purest of economic theory. Arrow and Debreu imagined a complete system of markets in which commodities are defined not only by their physical characteristics but also by the dates and contingencies — 'states of nature' — at which they are to be exchanged. Such a market, for example, would enable me to contract now for an umbrella on the day of the Harvard–Yale football game in 1990 if it is raining that day and if a Republican is in the White House. In exchange, I could sell a promise to give an economics lecture in New York City in 1994 if I am still in good health and the unemployment rate exceeds 8 per cent. Prices set in such markets would clear supplies and demands in advance for all such commodities, with each participant constrained by his or her budget to promise no more than he or she can deliver. Arrow and Debreu showed that this system would realize the claims for the economy-wide efficiency and optimality of competitive markets.

It can be shown further that securities and insurance markets can mimic the Arrow–Debreu system, provided that the menu of available securities 'spans' the space of 'states of nature'.[19] That is, there must be as many different independent securities as there are states of nature. I could get my umbrella with the proceeds of a security that would pay off in the medium of exchange under the specified contingencies at the time of the 1990 Harvard–Yale football game. At a price, I would be insured against those risks.

Our actual institutions fall far short of the Arrow–Debreu vision. There are good reasons. Markets require resources to operate; given their costs, it would be inefficient to have a complete set. Many of them would in any case be too thin to be competitive. 'States of nature' are difficult to define and observe. Lawyers and judges would be even busier than they already are on disputes over whether contingencies specified in contracts have occurred. Many relevant contingencies are not independent of the actions of the parties; as insurance carriers know, 'moral hazard' is a real problem.

Nevertheless the Arrow–Debreu ideal provides a useful way to look at our actual institutions and markets. The system does some things very well, for example, life and disability insurance, even health insurance. It enables individuals and families to trade earnings in their productive years for consumption in retirement and old age. Futures markets allow businesses and farmers to hedge against events that might alter spot prices of commodities they will be buying or selling. Capital markets enable fundamental risks of business enterprise to be taken by the adventurous, while risk-averters content with lower average returns are protected from many possible sources of loss.

Our financial system allows individuals and households considerable facilities to shift the time pattern of their spending and consumption to accord with their needs and preferences, rather than slavishly conforming to the time profile of their earnings. But it could do better.

For example, the long-term level payment mortgage was a great invention. But mortgage instruments with payments that conform more closely to typical earnings profiles and are flexible in maturity would be helpful to young families, especially in inflationary times. Likewise, older households whose equity in homes is the major part of net worth do not find it easy to consume such wealth while retaining occupancy and ownership. It should not be difficult to devise instruments which would meet their needs. Consumer credit also permits households to advance consumption in time and age, though at what seem exorbitant interest rates. Borrowing against future earnings, against human capital, is much more difficult than against negotiable financial or physical assets. Educational loans would not be generally available without government guarantees and subsidies. They could be longer in term, and lengths and even amounts of repayment could be contingent on the debtors' actual earnings.

The obvious major contingency which our system leaves uncovered is inflation. Twenty-five years ago we thought equities, which are, after all, titles to real capital goods and real returns earned by their use, were good hedges against inflation. Subsequent experience turned out otherwise, partly because inflation hit us from unexpected sources like OPEC, partly because policies to stem inflation lower profits and raise interest rates. Short-term nominal interest rates are better correlated with inflation; consequently variable interest instruments provide rough protection to both debtors and creditors. But the correlation is imperfect. It is not clear why private financial institutions cannot take the next step and develop price-indexed instruments for both savers and borrowers. Those institutions are better placed than the general public to assume the risks of deviations of interest rates from inflation rates. Of course, if the federal government were to issue indexed bonds — Her Majesty's Government has done so — it would be easy for financial intermediaries to offer indexed assets tailored in maturities and denominations to the needs of small savers.

The development of indexed financial instruments, with or without government initiative, would be facilitated by the construction of a price index more appropriate than the present consumer price index (CPI). This would exclude the effects of changes in the country's external terms of trade, from shocks to prices of oil or other imports and from movements in the foreign exchange value of the dollar. It would also exclude changes in indirect taxes. These CPI movements are essentially uninsurable for the nation as a whole. An index purged of them is preferable for wage contracts and social insurance benefits as well as for new financial instruments.

New financial markets and instruments have proliferated over the last decade, and it might be thought that the enlarged menu now spans more states of nature and moves us closer to the Arrow–Debreu ideal. Not much closer, I am afraid. The new options and futures contracts do not stretch very far into the future. They serve mainly to allow greater leverage to short-term speculators and abitrageurs, and to limit losses in one direction or the other. Collectively they contain considerable redundancy. Every financial market absorbs private resources to operate, and government resources to police. The country cannot afford all the markets that enthusiasts may dream up. In deciding whether to approve proposed contracts for trading, the authorities should consider whether they really fill gaps in the menu and enlarge the opportunities for Arrow–Debreu insurance, not just opportunities for speculation and financial arbitrage.

Functional efficiency

I turn finally to what I call *functional* efficiency, the services the financial industries perform for the economy as a whole.

Very few securities transactions are sales of new issues. They amounted to only $100 billion in 1983, and one-third of these were issues of financial businesses themselves.[20] Of the issues of non-financial corporations, a large share will have represented re-funding and restructuring of debt and equity rather than raising funds for new real investments. Even in recent years of high investment, 1978–9, 86 per cent of aggregate gross capital expenditures by non-financial corporations could have been financed by internal funds, retained after-tax earnings and depreciation. Retained earnings were in aggregate sufficient to cover two-thirds of investment net of capital consumption charges. In the recent recession, internal funds exceeded capital expenditures.[21]

These overall figures, it is true, understate the role of the capital markets. Some businesses with surpluses of internal funds over investment requirements finance the deficits of others, either directly by purchases of securities or, much more usually, indirectly via financial intermediaries. There are no statistics on the gross amount of this activity. However, suppose half of the new non-financial securities issues financed capital expenditures by deficit companies — this seems a conservatively high proportion. Then internal funds would be credited with two-thirds of gross 1978–9 capital expenditures instead of 86 per cent, and only with one-sixth of net capital expenditures instead of two-thirds. The calculations include as external funds bank loans and short-term paper, 68 per cent of the total, twice as much as the funds raised in securities and mortgage markets. They also include, on the investment side, corporate-owned residential structures and inventories.

What is clear is that very little of the work done by the securities industry, as gauged by the volume of market activity, has to do with the financing of real investment in any very direct way. Likewise, those markets have very little to do, in aggregate, with the translation of the savings of households into corporate business investment. That process occurs mainly outside the market, as retention of earnings gradually and irregularly augments the value of equity shares. Capital markets and financial intermediaries assist this process by facilitating transfers from surplus companies to deficit companies.

Financial markets, of course, play a much bigger role in financing public capital investments of state and local governments and government deficits in general. Through the markets government securities find their way into the portfolios of individuals and, more importantly, of financial intermediaries.

The traditional role of commercial banks is to facilitate the circulation of funds among businesses, channelling the temporary seasonal and short-run surpluses of some businesses to those businesses with temporary deficits. This circulation is closely connected with the diverse rhythms of accumulation and decumulation of inventories of finished goods, raw materials, and work in process, and of inter-business accounts receivable and payable. Some of the surpluses show up, almost automatically, in excess of bank deposits over borrowings from banks, while the deficit companies are drawing down their deposits and using more fully their lines of credit.

Banks' intermediaries between businesses is mixed with their borrowing from and lending to other types of economic agents — households, governments, and foreigners. As banking has become increasingly generalized, the word 'commercial' has become less appropriate. Likewise, other financial firms and institutions, new credit markets, and even non-financial companies have invaded both sides of the banks' traditional commercial intermediation business.

I have noted above that there is little net aggregate transfer of household saving into business investment. Indeed most household saving goes into household investments in residences and consumer durable goods. Commercial banks, savings institutions, insurance companies, and pension funds are vehicles for channelling the surpluses of some households to finance the deficits of others. This is done mainly by mortgage lending and by consumer credit. Since houses, in particular, are beyond the capacity of all but a very few families to purchase from current or accumulated savings, intermediation between surplus and deficit households is a great service to the economy.

A by-product of traditional commercial banking was the provision of a payments mechanism; checkable demand deposits became the predominant means of payment in modern economies. This function, too, is now increasingly shared with other financial institutions and businesses. The link between commercial banking, supplying money, and operating a payments mechanism was more a historical evolution than a planned design. It is logically possible to think of different arrangements, ranging from, on the one side, a public monopoly in the provision of this public good to complete deregulation and laissez-faire at the other extreme. We seem likely to stay in the middle of the spectrum, moving in the direction of deregulation.

Total debits to deposit accounts — check clearings, wire transfers, and so on — amount to more than $100 *trillion* a year. A dollar of demand deposits turns over an average of once a day. The bank-operated payments mechanism does a lot of work. From the fact that more than 40 per cent of national clearings are in New York City alone we may infer that more than half of cheque payments are for the financial transactions described above — the flip side of them, so to speak. Transactions directly connected with the flow of goods and services probably amount to no more than a quarter of aggregate debits.[22]

Our financial intermediaries are decentralized and competitive. But they hardly fit the textbook model of pure competition, where firms too small to affect prices compete in supplying homogeneous products. The applicable model is that provided 50 years ago by Edward Chamberlin, monopolistic competition.[23] Like Chamberlin's firms, banks and other financial intermediaries actively seek the custom of depositors and borrowers by trying to differentiate their products as well as by offering attractive interest rates and terms. Product differentiation takes many forms, among them locational convenience, comfortable premises, personal attention, packaging and advertising.

Symptoms of monopolistic competition are readily apparent. Like petrol stations clustered on the same intersections, competing banking offices are adjacent to each other. Like the products of those petrol stations, the financial services differ only trivially. To persuade us of the contrary, monopolistically competing firms resort to a great deal of advertising. In 1981, banks and savings institutions spent $158 million on local TV advertising. Financial advertising in newspapers of 64 cities amounted to $387 million, 5½ per cent of advertising other than classified.[24] Another symptom is the prevalence of conventional pricing based on the leadership of large firms in the industry — the prime rate is an obvious case in point.

Many optimistic advocates of financial deregulation attributed the 'wastes of monopolistic competition' — Chamberlin's phrase — to the legal ceilings on deposit interest rates. They correctly observed that banks and other intermediaries were led to fill the profitable gap between lending rates and those ceilings by advertising and non-price competition. They predicted that abolition of the ceilings would eliminate wasteful forms of competition. I doubt that, because the system remains monopolistically competitive even without the regulation of deposit interest and because deregulation itself vastly enlarges the opportunities for product differentiation. One side-effect of the regulations was to standardize the deposit instruments banks could offer. Since proliferation of non-standardized products is costly, beyond a certain point it is not necessarily a service to the consuming public.

In other countries, where branching and merging of banks and other financial enterprises are not restricted, the industry is highly concentrated. The United States is probably moving inexorably in this direction. The number of distinct firms, though not the number of offices, will shrink drastically. Competition will be oligopolistic rivalry rather than Chamberlinian monopolistic competition. There will be some economies of scale in the operations of the payments mechanisms, and some improvements in the management of small banks, which have comfortably enjoyed local monopolies sheltered by anti-branching laws. But there will be some losses too. The local commercial banker knew his community; at his best, he was a good judge of personal and business risks. Branches of large nation-wide lenders following bureaucratic rules are all too likely to deny credit to small new entrepreneurs while their national headquarters take immense billion-dollar risks with foreign countries and big-time operators.

Conclusions

Any appraisal of the efficiency of our financial system must reach an equivocal and uncertain verdict. In many respects, as I have tried to indicate, the system serves us as individuals and as a society very well indeed. As I have also tried to say, however, it does not merit complacency and self-congratulation either in the industry itself or in the academic professions of economics and finance. Nor are its shortcomings entirely attributable to government regulations and likely to disappear as deregulation proceeds apace. Here, as elsewhere, many regulations have been counterproductive. But the process of deregulation should be viewed neither as a routine application of free market philosophy nor as a treaty among conflicting sectoral interests. Rather it should be guided by sober pragmatic consideration of what we can reasonably expect the financial system to achieve and at what social cost. My lecture today presents some of the problems, but I regret I have no sovereign solution to propose.

I confess to an uneasy Physiocratic suspicion, perhaps unbecoming in an academic, that we are throwing more and more of our resources, including the cream of our youth, into financial activities remote from the production of goods and services, into activities that generate high private rewards disproportionate to their social productivity. I suspect that the immense power of the computer is being harnessed to this 'paper economy', not to do the same transactions more economically but to balloon the quantity and variety of financial exchanges. For this reason, perhaps, high technology has so far yielded disappointing results in economy-wide productivity. I fear that, as Keynes saw even in his day, the advantages of the liquidity and negotiability of financial instruments come at the cost of facilitating nth-degree speculation which is short-sighted and inefficient.

The casino aspect of our financial markets was the subject of a thoughtful and devastating article on commodity futures markets by John Train.[25] The author, himself in the investment business, pointed out that speculation in these contracts was a negative-sum game for the general public, thanks to the large 'win' of the brokers, estimated at several billions of dollars annually. Only 5 per cent of the contracts exchanged entail actual deliveries of the commodities. Train berated brokerage houses for misleading amateur clients into this particular casino.

The case points out the general dilemma. Commodity futures contracts serve a significant Arrow–Debreu function for traders with business interests in the commodity; and since hedging will seldom balance supply and demand, some risk-takers, speculators, are needed in the market, too. But Arrow and Debreu did not have continuous sequential trading in mind; when that occurs, as Keynes noted, it attracts short-horizon speculators and middlemen, and distorts or dilutes the influence of fundamentals on prices. I suspect that Keynes was right to suggest that we should provide greater deterrents to transient holdings of financial instruments and larger rewards for long-term investors.

Notes

1. *New York Times*, 2 May 1984, p. D1. The representation of financial executives would be larger except that a corporation is required to disclose compensation only for its five highest-paid officials. The *Wall Street Journal*, 21 May 1984, p. 33, guessed that as many as 15–20 officials of Phibro-Salamon, in addition to the five listed, would have been eligible. Furthermore, most Wall Street firms are partnerships or private corporations and do not report. The *Journal* said it was 'a safe bet' that the senior executives or partners of several leading firms belonged on the list, very likely at the top.
2. Information on job placements from the School's office of Career Planning and Placement; categorization of positions by the author.
3. Recent names in the news include William Silber and Fisher Black, who left New York University and Massachusetts Institute of Technology respectively. Many others, who have not made the full leap, serve as consultants. They serve not only during vacations from classes; a day a week free for consultation during terms is standard in business schools.
4. K. Arrow and G. Debreu, 'Existence of an Equilibrium for a Competitive Economy', *Econometrica*, vol. 22, 1954, pp. 256–90. See also Debreu, *Theory of Value, An Axiomatic Analysis of Economic Equilibrium*, New York, 1959.
5. Figures from US National Income and Product Accounts Tables, *Survey of Current Business*, US Department of Commerce, July 1983.
6. The 9 per cent assumes the same proportion between direct and indirect expenses on labour and capital as estimated in the 1972 input–output table for the US economy. See 'The Input–Output Structure of the US Economy 1972'

and 'Dollar Value Tables for the 1972 Input–Output Study', *Survey of Current Business*, February and April 1979.

7. Figures derived from statistical reports in *SEC Monthly Review*, US Securities and Exchange Commission, and from *1983 Fact Book*, New York Stock Exchange.

8. Figures based on *Federal Reserve Bulletin*, July 1983, Table A.1, p. 501.

9. Figures from *'83 Savings and Loan Sourcebook*, US League of Savings Institutions, and *1982 Fact Book of Savings Banking*, National Association of Mutual Savings Banks.

10. Alfred Cowles, 'Can Stock Market Forecasters Forecast?'. *Econometrica*, vol. 1, 1933, pp. 309–24; Alfred Cowles and Herbert E. Jones, 'Some A Posteriori Probabilities in Stock Market Action', *Econometrica*, vol. 5, 1937, pp. 280–94.

11. Burton G Malkiel, *A Random Walk down Wall street*, New York, 1973; John G. Cragg and Burton G. Malkiel, *Expectations and the Structure of Share prices*, Chicago, 1982.

12. Robert J. Shiller, 'Do Stock Prices Move Too Much to be Justified by Subsequent Changes in Dividends?', *American Economic Review*, vol. 71, 1981, pp. 421–36.

13. Robert J. Shiller, 'The Volatility of Long-term Interest Rates and Expectations Models of the Term Structure', *Journal of Political Economy*, vol. 87, 1979, pp. 1190–219.

14. Stephen S. Golub, 'Exchange Rate Variability: Is it Excessive', Chapter 4 of unpublished Ph.D dissertation, 'International Financial Markets, Oil Prices, and Exchange Rates', Yale University, 1983.

15. William C. Brainard, J.B. Shoven, and L. Weiss, 'The Financial Valuation of the Return to Capital', *Brookings Papers on Economic Activity*, no. 2, 1980, pp. 453–502.

16. Franco Modigliani and R. Cohn, 'Inflation, Rational Valuation and the Market', *Journal of Business, University of Chicago*, vol. 35, pp. 24–44.

17. This and the quotations and paraphrases that follow come from Keynes's *General Theory of Employment, Interest and Money*, New York, 1936, pp. 156–60. The whole of his Chapter 12, 'The State of Long-term Expectation' deserves reading and rereading by anyone interested in these subjects.

18. James Tobin, 'A Proposal for International Monetary Reform', *Eastern Economic Journal*, vol. 4, 1978, pp. 153–9.

19. Roy Radner, 'Competitive Equilibrium under Uncertainty', *Econometrica*, vol. 36, 1968, pp. 31–58.

20. Figures on new issues from *SEC Monthly Review*.

21. Figures for 'Sources and Uses of Funds, Nonfarm Nonfinancial Corporate Business', from the Board of Governors of the Federal Reserve System, published *inter alia*, in *Economic Report of the President*, Washington, DC, 1984, Table B-87, p. 320.

22. Statistics of Bank Debits and Deposit Turnover are published monthly in the *Federal Reserve Bulletin*, Table 1.20.

23. Edward Chamberlin, *The Theory of Monopolistic Competition*, Cambridge, MA, 1933.

24. *Statistical Abstract of the United States*, 1982–3, Tables 966–8, pp. 567–8.

25. John Train, *New York Times*, 12 May 1984.

9 The dollar and the world economy: the case for concerted management

Harold Lever

Conventional wisdom has been strained past breaking-point in seeking to explain both the excessive weakness of the dollar in the mid-1970s and its excessive strength so far in the 1980s. In the 1970s there were loud criticisms from both Europe and the USA that the dollar's weakness was due to misguided American government policies. It was repeatedly asserted that the dollar would cease being weak only if the USA 'put its house in order'. Now, seven or eight years later, even more alarming policies are said to have produced the opposite situation — a dollar which is by common consent grossly overvalued. The paradox is that the USA is now being told to do much the same thing as before, but this time in order to produce the opposite effect. Much of this advice, as is normal on these occasions, has a moralizing overtone. In my view it is wise to defer the sermons until we have examined the actual market operations of the dollar more closely than is habitual.

In looking at recent history to discover the 'mystery' of dollar movements, we must first highlight certain delusions which hold an undeserved sway, not only in the popular mind but also in what would normally be thought authoritative quarters, all over the world. These delusions are:

1. That the dollar's rise is an expression of the relative competence of countries and their governments. As the Japanese yen has experienced deformities not very different from the other currencies it is difficult to see how this absurdity can be maintained.
2. That high American interest rates, whether resulting from the fiscal deficit or not, produced a surge of investment money from abroad between 1982 and 1984 which was responsible for the dollar's rise.

Lord Lever was Chancellor of the Duchy of Lancaster 1974–79. He was Chairman of the Commonwealth Group of Experts, appointed by the Commonwealth Heads of Government in 1983, to report on the debt problem. This article is a revised version of the Fred Hirsch Memorial Lecture given in New York on 14 May 1985. It first appeared in *Lloyds Bank Review*, no. 157, July 1985.

3. That speculators are responsible for the dollar's rise.
4. That the damage being caused by grossly misaligned exchange rates is unavoidable and that nothing can be done about it.

I will argue that the explanation for the dollar's movements is to be found in the supply and demand equation of dollars in the currency markets: that capital movements have become by far the dominant influence on the supply and demand for dollars and that the movement of bank money is the most mobile aspect of capital movements. I will also argue that the movements in bank money arise from the normal and desirable functioning of the dollar as the world currency.

I will further argue that though the turnover in the currency markets is enormous, virtually all of it is self-balancing froth. What matters is not the total dealings but the balance of supply and demand. I will argue that this balance would be manageable if we had concerted intervention by central banks. Unfortunately, under our present unmanaged floating rate arrangements, it is capital movements and not fundamental economic factors which determine the parity of the dollar. I will point out that this leaves us with an unmistakable choice. We must either pursue co-operative action to provide some counterbalance to capital movements or accept the continued damage to the fundamental workings of the world economy.

Under floating exchange rates, the movement of the dollar parity at any given time will depend on the balance between the supply and demand of dollars at the existing parity. The main sources of supply and demand for dollars are: the condition of the current account of the balance of payments; movements of medium and long-term portfolio and investment funds; speculative movements; and banking movements. When we examine the changes in these categories between the period of dollar weakness in the 1970s and its recent period of great strength, the most striking contrast is the extent to which the supply of dollars has been increased by the deterioration of the current account balance of the USA. Yet instead of going down under the vast extra supply of dollars thus created, the dollar has risen sharply. Clearly there must have been sustained counterbalancing change elsewhere in the supply and demand equation for dollars even to maintain the previous parity level. Water does not run uphill even in currency markets. Something has tilted the supply–demand balance.

The first question must be: Has there been a great inflow of money converted from other currencies seeking to benefit from the high American interest rates? In markets, in which a year's interest can be lost in an adverse currency change of a few days, it is expectations of parity changes, rather than interest rate differentials, which dominate external currency movements. It is, therefore, on the face of it, in the highest degree unlikely that any rise in the American interest rates, especially one associated with fiscal disorder, could prompt so great an inflow as to outweigh the growing trade deficit of the last two years. The existence of a surge in such investment funds has been asserted or assumed without proof in innumerable comments. In fact, the official figures show no major change in inward investment between 1982 and 1984. And, despite certainties in aspects of these figures, it can be safely asserted that there has been no change in foreign investment between 1982 and 1984 which could conceivably have outweighed the $100 billion increase in the current account deficit.

I now turn to speculative movements. They find expression in a number of not readily identifiable ways. But, it is impossible to believe that they could autonomously be so perverse as to outweigh the adverse factors facing the dollar, including the sheer weight of dollars generated by the American trade deficit. Indeed why on earth should speculators have supposed that the dollar would go up when all expert comment suggested the contrary especially when, from the speculator's point of view, the increased current account deficit was threatening the supply–demand equation of dollars at its most vulnerable point? I must emphasize that I am not suggesting that speculation has not contributed to the dollar's deformities. Still less do I believe that speculative movements have helped to dampen the dollar's swings. The reverse is the case. Most speculators seek to win profits (or more commonly to avoid losses) by anticipating the continuation of a trend, not its reversal. Far from fighting the dollar's downward trend in the late 1970s, for example, speculators followed it and thereby added to the dollar's undervaluation. The same, in reverse, has happened in the 1980s. There is nothing exceptional in this behaviour. The only people who are surprised by it are those who accepted the academic case for floating rates in the 1960s and 1970s. This was based on seminar models which either ignored or assumed away the problems they would create. The key false assumption which was made was that any major deformity of a currency's parity caused, for example, by cyclical capital movements, would be corrected by the action of long-sighted speculators.

Outside the seminar it should have been obvious that anything resembling unmanaged floating rates would be dominated, destructively and irrelevantly, by short-term and medium-term capital movements and by seasonal and cyclical trading and payments movements. Market traders and speculators behave in exactly the opposite way to the seminar assumptions. The reality of free money markets is that the overwhelming weight of speculative movement will (rightly from the trader's point of view) be concerned to follow an immediate trend, not to oppose it. Nobody will sell the dollar at a given time in the opinion that it will be lower next year if he thinks he can sell at a higher price in the next hour, next day, next week or next month. Any experienced currency trader will tell you that speculators who take a long-term view usually end up in bankruptcy well before their 'long-term view' has been proved true or false.

In my view, therefore, the recent strength of the dollar is partly to be explained by speculative transactions but these should be seen as 'piggy back' transactions, that is, as riding on the back of other more fundamental forces.

We must therefore consider banking movements. First, a little history. Before, during and after Bretton Woods, the role of the dollar in financing world trade increased. The American banking system, and, linked to it, the dollar operations of banks throughout the world, has taken on the lion's share of satisfying the world's needs for funds in addition to the domestic needs of the USA itself. So, in the years immediately following 1974, after the first oil shock, American banks, with overseas banks which increasingly attached themselves to the dollar banking system, poured out hundreds of billions of dollars in loans to finance the deficits of South American and other governments and to finance third-party trade, that is, trading transactions all over the world between countries other than the USA itself. This lending seemed safe, profitable and was warmly encouraged by all the leading governments. By these means, the dollar performed its functions as the world currency. Without these vast credits the world recession after 1974 would have been calamitous. There were important errors by the governments and banks in the method of recycling the OPEC dollars, but there could be no doubt that the world economy was saved from great injury by the actions of the world banking system. It was a productive error.

This process injected enormous supplies of dollars into the market. Most of these dollars were subsequently changed for Deutschmarks, yen, Swiss francs and sterling, in the ordinary course of trade. They were, therefore, added to the existing overhang of dollars on the world market that stemmed from American overseas investment after the war. On this there had been a good deal of public comment — in fact, it helped to bring about the demise of the Bretton Woods system.

The world recovery in the 20 years after the war transformed the dollar situation. The post-war dollar shortage changed to an emerging glut. This was caused not by the trading surplus of the recovering countries but by the accumulation of dollars resulting from American overseas investment. The weight of this outflow made it inevitable that the ability of the USA to deliver gold in exchange for foreign-held dollars, as provided by Bretton Woods, could not be maintained. By 1967 the gold option, though formally still extant, had in practice ceased to exist. The world then had for the first time to face head on the key question of capital movements, to which Bretton Woods had given only a temporary and unclear answer.

At Bretton Woods and thereafter, everybody agreed that parities ought to reflect economic fundamentals, including long-term direct investment.

Everyone agreed that parities should not be decided or distorted by capital movements. Bretton Woods provided a satisfactory answer to this problem as long as there was a dollar shortage. The dollar shortage ended sooner than anybody expected and was replaced by what was then thought to be a dollar glut. It was not really much of a glut, but the revival of the European economies was accompanied by a revival of European nationalist self-assertion. It was resented that American citizens could buy into Europe and pay in dollars to do so. The immense benefits accruing to Europe from this were little considered. What we heard were the vigorous assertions of national pride which were in principle no different from those which now keep investment capital from many less sophisticated developing countries, the folly of which the Europeans now join in deploring.

With the removal of the gold option, the countries in dollar surplus were greatly troubled by the question: what does a country do when capital movements produce more dollars than the central bank is willing to hold? Should it attempt to restrict the capital movements which brought this about? Should it let its parity rise to a point where the market will absorb or deter the unwanted dollars or should it, on its own responsibility, reluctantly and carrying the parity risk, hold them without limit? For a time, surplus countries alternated uneasily and resentfully between these choices. Gold worshippers to a man — some more noisily than others — they felt greatly frustrated by the closing of the gold option.

It was not only the surplus countries which chafed under the restraints and disciplines involved in maintaining a proclaimed but adjustable parity: countries not affected directly by the dollar glut saw in the situation the chance for them, too, to escape from these constraints in the belief that they would achieve greater freedom in formulating their own economic policies. They joined the surplus countries in seeking to break down the Bretton Woods arrangements. They all saw in this breakdown an ending of 'the exorbitant privilege' which enabled the USA to settle its payments deficits in its own currency. They all believed that the ending of the Bretton Woods arrangements would reduce the dominance of the dollar in the world economy.

The USA also became attracted to this attitude because it saw in the breakdown the opportunity of devaluing the dollar and thereby removing both its relatively small trading deficit and the formal obligation to deliver gold against dollars, which embarrassingly it was no longer able to fulfil. In short, all the great countries, for different reasons, were determined to replace a multilaterally agreed system for world currencies with a regression to unilateralist action in the mistaken belief that thereby they would not only painlessly solve the problems of trading imbalances but also the problems of capital movements.

The prospectus which sold an *unmanaged* floating rate was false at almost every relevant point. Unsurprisingly, its practice brutally disappointed the expectations of the world's leaders who accepted it. It has not removed trading imbalances; it has exaggerated them, especially those of the USA. Above all, it has not produced parities which broadly reflect economic fundamentals but volatile parities grossly distorted up and down by capital movements.

In their regression to unilateralism none of these professing multilateralists were willing to see the problem of capital movements correctly. They were all agreed that it was neither feasible nor desirable to attempt to impose effective controls upon them. But they refused to see that in the new situation, the dollar in its role of world currency had become a world responsibility. There have to be procedures agreed between the leading countries to discharge this responsibility, which would ensure that benign' and necessary capital movements could continue without disrupting parities. Instead of answering the problem, our leaders sought to run away from it by moving to floating rates. In fact they had unwittingly decided to accept the chronically disrupted parities inevitable in the absence of some systematic multilateral management of the dollar in its world currency role.

In the period from 1974 to the end of 1978, the more or less continuous outflow of dollars on capital account was the underlying reason for the sustained weakness of the dollar. This weakness could have been avoided only by systematic central bank intervention, such as would have been provided if Bretton Woods had been brought up to date instead of being destroyed. But there was little comprehension of the true reasons for the dollar's decline, and therefore little motivation to check it by multilateral action. Benign neglect became the order of the day — abdication of responsibility in the area of capital movements and their impact on parities. Such intellectual energy as our leaders were able to muster was devoted to mutual recrimination and sermonizing, with none left to see the problem straight or to tackle it. They were like car drivers involved in an accident, charging each other with careless driving when in truth the collision was caused because none of the cars involved possessed an effective braking system.

In late 1978 the government of the USA, in co-operation with those of other major countries, was driven to mount the largest intervention package in history. Though only a fraction of this package was deployed, its announcement steadied the dollar. As the large speculative position began to be reversed, a breathing space was given to the dollar and in 1979 its value was more realistically maintained. So much for the parrot cry that intervention is always ineffective. With the new realism about the dollar, investment flows into the USA started to grow: by 1981 they had reached *$80 billion*, and they continued thereafter at about the same level. These flows counterbalanced the outward dollar flows from the banks which continued apace until 1982.

The early 1980s saw the growth of anxieties about the wisdom, safety and desirability of some of the international financing which had earlier been undertaken. In particular, the banking crisis made its impact. The outflow of dollars from the banking system was sharply reduced. This, together with reduced American investment and profit-taking from the closing and reversing of speculative bear positions, laid the foundation for the stronger dollar and put it on an upward trend.

It should here be noted that the huge accumulated outflow from the earlier period had by this time mainly been converted into other currencies. But most of it still remained as obligations to American creditors denominated in dollars. Any recall by creditors would henceforth require debtors to achieve repayment or service by converting their own currencies into dollars, a process which when it occurred would inevitably drive those currencies down and the dollar up.

Between 1982 and 1984 the inflow of foreign money into the dollar increased hardly at all. But the capital balance of the USA in this period improved dramatically because of the sharp drop in American private lending overseas. According to the official figures, which are known to be incomplete and which understate the drop, bank lending fell from over $100 billion in 1982 to virtually nothing in 1984, partly, but only partly, because of the debt crisis. This contrasts with a deterioration in the American current account of *$90 billion*.

It is this dramatic change in the American capital account which has been the lead factor in the sustained rise of the dollar parity. It has overwhelmed even the large increase in the supply of dollars caused by the astronomical increase in the American trade deficit. The upward trend, once established, in its turn attracted a speculative entourage which added further to the upward pressure on the dollar parity.

From all this we must now draw the following conclusions:

1. Vast movements of dollar funds are an inevitable consequence of the dollar's role as the world currency. Massive changes in the dollar banking system's posture are neither encouraged nor deterred by parity changes because the obligations to the banks are for the most part continuously denominated in dollars. But changes in the American capital account trends, to which speculative movements and to a less volatile extent investment movements attach themselves, produce violent and unpredictable swings in parity levels. The dramatic turnaround in bank money movements was triggered by the debt crisis but other factors played a part, too. The mainspring, however, was a sudden and belated realization of the dangers in the overseas lending to which the banks had exposed themselves.
2. In the absence of systematic and concerted intervention to balance these cyclical movements, the parity of the dollar in its relation to every

major currency in the world will be deformed. It is cash on the table which talks in markets not rhetoric or analysis, especially as much of the latter is offered after the event.

3. These movements will not be corrected by the action of speculators taking a long-term view.

The deformities of the dollar have already been damaging for economies throughout the world. They create major distortions in trade, in investment flows, in manufacturing patterns, in agricultural and commodity prices. As Paul Volcker rightly said in the first of these lectures in 1978: 'When patterns of trade or capital become influenced by monetary fluctuations rather than lasting comparative advantage, the underlying rationale of a liberal trade and investment order is undercut . . . . The instinctive political reaction in the face of seemingly capricious impacts on one industry or another is to protect or subsidize domestic industry, or to impede the flow of capital.'[1]

The problem of capital movements the world's leaders have evaded for 20 years must now be squarely faced. What, then, are we to do? Professor McKinnon[2] and others have suggested that the remedy would be to target American monetary policy on the exchange rate. Judgements on interest rates, and so on, would have to be related not to the needs of the American domestic economy but to the need to repel or to attract foreign money. In my view such action cannot succeed in its objective but the major distortions which would result even from the attempt would cause further serious injury to the USA and to the world economy.

Another course of action would be to seek to impose restrictions on the free movement of bank finance and investment capital. This is neither feasible nor desirable. Of course, a better regulatory system internationally for banks is quite another matter. This leaves the world's leaders with two choices. They can either accept the profoundly disruptive consequences of a dollar parity unrelated to relevant fundamentals or organize the concerted action required broadly to neutralize the impact of movements in banking money on parities. I here return to Paul Volcker's first lecture: 'International money, any more than domestic, will not manage itself!'[3]

I accept that there is no immediate prospect other than to work within the broad framework of the present floating arrangements. For the immediate future I would strongly support Paul Volcker's plea that there should be a firm understanding between the leading nations that they will strongly resist extremes of fluctuations by concerted intervention. I agree, too, with him that a sense that extreme fluctuations will be resisted and reversed could help to stabilize market expectations and thus reduce the risk of these fluctuations developing in the first place.

Though there is a case for greater harmonization of the economic and financial policies of the leading countries, I do not believe that the kind of intervention for which I am calling should or can await further achievements in that direction. Indeed, greater currency stability is more a precondition of advance in this area, while harmonization by itself will not eliminate the problem of capital movements. I am most definitely not calling for intervention to defend unrealistic parities. What I am calling for is intervention to counterbalance the mechanical deforming effect of those money movements which are not in themselves related to the fundamental economic factors which ought to govern parity but are produced by the normal functioning of the dollar as the world currency. Nor am I perfectionist in my approach. I would be satisfied to remedy the grosser distortions which arise from the patent defects in the present monetary arrangements. The concerted intervention that I am urging is the minimum necessary financial hygiene required for the functioning of the dollar as the world currency.

The choice before us is not whether we have some other world currency but whether we have a better functioning of the dollar in that role. We must not allow the distant prospect of some other noble but purely notional goal to lose for us the more modest prizes offered by immediate reality. Most countries maintain an Exchange Equalization Fund. What I am calling for is the systematic co-ordination of these Funds on the required scale to bring into being what in effect would be a world Exchange Equalization Fund.

The central banks' operations should be based on the realities of today's money world and on a recognition of the dollar's unique role in it. This role was not an artificial construct of Bretton Woods or any formal procedures — it derived naturally from the strength, stability and dynamism of the economy of the USA and the unique size, depth and openness of its money markets.

The central position of the USA in the world economy and in the world's financial markets will mean that in the years ahead it will be a magnet for great quantities of world money and normally the world's biggest capital importer. But it will also be the world's biggest capital exporter thanks to the dynamism and world range of its entrepreneurs and bankers.

These two-way flows of capital — short-, medium- and long-term — are a desirable feature of the modern world economy; indeed, they are necessary to its vigour and dynamics. But they will reflect and respond to events world-wide and to the rhythms and hazards of the world scene. These two-way flows will over a long period find a broadly desirable balance but not in the short or medium run. There will be phases when they will be sharply out of balance. We have been in such a phase since 1981. Import of capital continues to be buoyant but export of capital has dried up in large part, but by no means solely, due to the international banking crisis. These phases are an inevitable aspect of the role of the USA in the world economy and especially of the functioning of the dollar as the world currency. If no counterbalancing action is available large capital surpluses and deficits will be created for the USA and market action will automatically force the dollar up or down as the case may be. Large matching trading deficits or surpluses will result and because these derive not from the normal functionings of competitiveness and long-term comparative advantage but from monetary consequences of the fluctuations in the US capital account, they will be difficult to correct and will have a capricious and disruptive impact on trade, capital direction, employment and, ultimately, on political relationships.

The only way of avoiding these haphazard dislocations of the American and the world economy is by pursuing co-operative intervention in the exchange markets to balance the American capital account otherwise than solely by trade imbalances. Bretton Woods broadly provided this kind of intervention, but it was not adapted to world post-war recovery. Unlike Bretton Woods, the interventions I am advocating would allow parities to fluctuate, but within a range determined by market forces freed from dominance of an uncorrected capital imbalance. We will get a truer market sufficiently responding to fundamental economic factors, not the false market of recent years reflecting mainly the phases of sharp disparity in American inward and outward capital flows.

Unlike Bretton Woods and most unilateral interventions the concerted central bank intervention would be directed not to maintaining an artificial or unrealistic parity but to creating the market conditions for a realistic one. There might at times be many billions involved in these interventions but any such sums would be trivial compared with the size of the world gross product which is being protected. This is now running at over \$12 trillion a year. They would be tiny even when compared with one year's normal growth in world gross production of around \$400 billion. And it is not only a year's growth that is being threatened by present currency instability.

Contrary to such misguided talk of 'spending' billions on intervention or 'pouring money down the drain', no money is spent, it is exchanged. If concerted intervention had begun in the early 1980s the Fed would now possess larger amounts of a range of currencies, while other central banks would own more dollars. We would have witnessed a productive rearrangement of the currency reserves of the central banks. That is why talk of an inflationary increase in the money supply is misguided, too. No new money is created. When you sell dollars you acquire Deutschmarks, yen and sterling. The effect on the global money supply is precisely zero. And it is time that governments woke up to the fact that it is a global money supply with which we are dealing. When in the fraction of a second an electric impulse turns a yen or Deutschmark or pound into a dollar or vice versa, calculations based on the amount of money held in a particular currency at a particular time are plainly absurd.

It will be argued that any co-operative intervention that is politically feasible could be and would be outweighed by market forces. The gross turnover of currency dealings should not dazzle or mislead us as to the size of the task that is involved in the currency correction system I am advocating. It is not the total buying or selling orders of the day that decides the parity, it is the balance between them. It is that margin of excess or shortfall in demand for the dollar at the existing parity which determines in which direction the parity will go. We are too little informed abut the extent of that excess or shortfall at any given period, nor is it easy to assess what margin produces what parity change. We can, however, be certain that the margin of excess or shortfall is a minuscule fraction of the total turnover, which overwhelmingly consists of self-balancing short-term trading. Even the longer-term movements have a substantial element of self-balance. In no period has it been beyond the power of the central banks to cope. The ability to act is there, but the willingness to act will only come when governments of the world achieve a correct understanding of the problem.

The options open are unmistakable. Governments must either permit their central banks to organize systematic intervention to balance the effect on parity of the movement of bank funds or they must allow these movements to continue to operate unchecked as the crucial determinant of dollar parity. The future path of the dollar has become unpredictable and also that of the American trading deficit which is affected by it. Equally the dollar parity will greatly affect the outcome of the world debt problem for which no coherent or convincing solution has yet been proposed. The dollar trading deficit must be corrected. This cannot be done without a correction of the dollar parity. Even with this, correction will be difficult and require a good deal of time. While it continues it distorts investment, production and employment in the USA and promotes protectionist forces. Those countries whose export trade is temporarily benefited by the deficit will find that the inevitable correction will result in serious future dislocation of the industrial structures their export boom is producing. A 'soft landing' for the dollar parity is at best a hopeful outside chance. Without action on the lines I have advocated we run the most terrible risks of disruptive disorder in the dollar parity and thereby in the parities of every other major country's currency.

To sum up, the dollar's role as the world currency implies normal and desirable flows of bank finance which, under the present floating rate arrangements, must inevitably result in cycles of gross parity deformity. We must either find the means broadly to counterbalance the effect of these movements or we will continue to experience, at an accelerating pace and to an ever more dangerous degree, those trends that have already severely disrupted the progress of interdependent prosperity and now threaten a major assault upon the central principles on which the successful post-war liberal trading experience was based.

Notes

1. See p. 67–68.
2. R. Mckinnon, *An International Standard for Monetary Stabilization*, Institute for International Economics, Washington, DC, 1984.
3. See p. 68.

10   Growth in the affluent society

Tibor Scitovsky

Faith in automatic market forces that push our economy towards full employment requires a hefty amount of optimism. Expressed in professional language, the model of self-adjusting full-employment equilibrium depends on several assumptions whose validity is questionable. The weakness of one of those assumptions, known as Say's law, has been pointed out by Keynes, who not only exposed its doubtful validity and argued the possibility of underemployment equilibrium but tried to do something about it.

Today, the failure of Keynesian policies to deal with our more complex problems has, in some mysterious way, restored many economists' faith in the existence of full-employment equilibrium. I have never been able to understand the logic of that. Surely, if Keynesian policies are no longer adequate, the natural thing to conclude would be that different or additional policies are needed. Perhaps Say's law was not the only unrealistic assumption to have lulled earlier generations of economists into their belief in a self-adjusting full-employment equilibrium.

I am proposing to take a critical look at another one of those questionable assumptions. I have in mind the long-held belief that when rising labour productivity makes it possible to produce the existing output with less labour, the workers made redundant will always find employment elsewhere, because the employed population will spend more out of its now higher income; and its increased spending will raise effective demand sufficiently to cause those workers to be re-employed in the production of the additional output demanded.

Underlying that belief is the implicit assumption that consumers' demand is insatiable, in the sense that when given more money, they always want to buy more goods and services, however many they may have already. Perhaps that was a reasonable enough assumption to make

Tibor Scitovsky is Professor Emeritus at Stanford University. This article is based on the Fred Hirsch Memorial Lecture given in London on 7 October 1986. It first appeared in *Lloyds Bank Review*, no. 163, January 1987. The author is grateful to Professors M. Abramowite, L. Tarshis, A.K. Sen and J. Steindl for their many constructive criticisms and suggestions.

in past centuries; but is it still justified in today's advanced economies, with their very much higher standards of living?

That the assumption may cease to be justified sooner or later is suggested by the fact that man's basic needs and desires for material comforts are satiable. You only have to look around you at all the people who are dieting and jogging to realize that, with respect to some needs at least, a large part of the advanced countries' populations have not only reached but passed the point of satiety.

The early neo-classical economists took for granted the satiability of wants and enshrined it in their law of the diminishing marginal utility of money; but that law got lost when the profession abandoned the assumption of measurable utility.

Marshall and his pupils seem to be just about the only twentieth-century economists to have confronted head on the question of satiability of wants. They answered it by classifying man's needs and desires into separate groups, of which the one that related to man's personal needs and comforts they considered the subject of satiable demand; whereas the group that had to do with the social comforts of distinction and superiority they considered the subject of insatiable demand — as if they had sensed that people's demand has to be insatiable for something to keep economic progress going, and believed to have found that something in social comfort. Was that belief justified, and if it was, is it still justified today?

To answer those questions, one must first of all note that ambiguity of the term 'insatiable demand'. Usually, we interpret it to mean *unlimited* demand, which keeps on rising with the rise in incomes; but it could also mean *unfillable* demand for something whose available supply cannot be increased for some reason and is not enough fully to satisfy the demand for it. Note that it is unlimited demand that stimulates the economy and serves as its engine of growth; unfillable demand merely raises prices but does not stimulate the economy. It makes a great deal of difference, therefore, whether people's demand for the sources of social comfort is insatiable in one or the other of those two senses.

To begin with, people's desire for distinction and superior status is unfillable, because to make some people feel superior, there must be others who are inferior to them, which means that not everybody can be superior, although at the bottom of his heart everybody or almost everybody would like to be.

Fortunately, the same is not quite and not always true of that other important source of social comfort, the symbols of status. The demand for them may be either unlimited or unfillable, depending on the nature of the particular status symbols people want.

In the poor societies of the past, whose populations often did not have enough to eat and lacked many of the material comforts, the rich and mighty usually made their superior status known by the lavish use of the material goods that others had to go without; and since they tried to outdo one another in the extravagance of their clothes and the magnificence and size of their meals, houses and retinues, there was no limit to the escalation of luxury.

If all that seemed outrageously wasteful and morally reprehensible, it did provide employment and livelihood to a lot of people; and it must have been a universal practice, to judge by the many sumptuary laws designed to curb its excesses and enacted by just about every past civilization. Earlier generations of economists therefore had good reason to pin their hopes for sustained economic growth on people's unlimited demand for conspicuous consumption.

Since then, however, the situation has changed. Increased sophistication, the sobering effect of the French Revolution, and the rise of puritanism have curbed the extravagance of the rich and made them adopt much less flamboyant status symbols. To appreciate the extent of that change recall our moral indignation when we learned of the Napoleonic pomp President Bokassa surrounded himself with, or about Michèle Duvalier's truckload of Valentino dresses and Imelda Marcos's 3,000 pairs of shoes. Yet, their lifestyle was merely a throwback to earlier times when such lavish extravagance was generally taken for granted as part of most rulers' standard behaviour.

What then is the new style and fashion in status symbols? To begin with, a person's income itself has come to be looked upon as a measure of the value that society puts on his services; and that causes him to appreciate a high income for its own sake, quite independently of how much of it he can spend. There is plenty of evidence to show that modern men and women are more anxious to earn money than to spend it and keep accumulating wealth whether or not they have any use for it.

Second, the outward display of high income and wealth has also changed its character. Affluent people today increasingly spend, not so much on more goods as on more exceptional ones, whose outstanding nature matches and symbolizes their own superior status, and with whose eventual donation for public use the very rich can further reassert and advertise their status. For there are many goods even in our mass-production economy that are unique, cannot be duplicated, are limited in supply or at least sufficiently outstanding from similar goods that they can be ranked against them in terms of quality, rarity, beauty, or excellence of design, just as people can be ranked according to their status. The public instinctively recognizes that such goods lend distinction to their owners and so are ideally suited for serving as status symbols.

The use of exceptional objects as badges of exceptional status is logical enough; but by abandoning the flamboyant status symbols of the past in favour of the subdued and sophisticated status symbols of the present, the rich and affluent have changed also the nature of their demand for badges of superiority. That demand was unlimited before; it has become unfillable now. For just as the availability of superior status is never enough to satisfy all those who want it, so the supply of outstanding and exceptional objects suitable to symbolize high status is also inherently scarce and insufficient fully to satisfy all the demand for them.

The peculiar nature of those goods, their increasing share in the affluent consumers' budget, and many of the problems created by the unfillable demand for them have been analysed with great perception by Fred Hirsch, whose memory we celebrate here today. He put all goods and services into one of two groups, which he called the *material* and the *positional* economies. The material economy contains all the goods and services whose supply can be increased either by using more labour and capital or by increasing the productivity of labour and capital. By contrast, the positional economy contains goods and services whose supply is inherently scarce, being limited in some absolute or socially imposed sense and therefore impossible to augment through increased productivity. That is why rising demand for them merely raises their prices or degrades their quality and occasionally raises their costs but does not call forth additional supply. He called these positional goods and services, perhaps because so many of them are used to symbolize their owners' position and rank in society.

Hirsch's favourite example of positional goods was the second houses well-to-do people own, in beautiful country locations, on the seashore, or in the form of picturesque former farmhouses, stately mansions or feudal castles. Indeed, they — along with paintings by dead masters and other antique art objects — are the best examples of positional goods, because their fixed supply is so very evident.

A more general and more important example, however, is the distinctive quality of a person's home that transforms it from a mere shelter into a highly visible symbol of his status, which is imparted to it by its good location, its elegance, and by the beauty and rarity of the art objects and furnishings it contains. That distinctive quality, therefore, must be considered the positional component of a house that is added on to its material component represented by its convenience and comfort as a shelter.

Note that while the Cambridge economists focused on the demand side when they distinguished the public's satiable demand for personal comforts from its insatiable desire for social comforts, Hirsch's two categories constitute a supply-side classification. His positional economy, however, has a large overlap with the sources of social comfort, although not all sources of social comfort are in the positional sector and not all positional goods and services are sources of social comfort. Examples of goods and services contained in the overlap include the examples already mentioned, outstanding objects created by established craftsmen and artists, as well as such things as exotic holidays and the best tables in the most fashionable restaurants.

In the following, I shall mainly focus on that overlap and draw your attention to an important consequence of the public's unfillable demand for positional goods, which Fred Hirsch in his short life had no time to explore.

After that long but necessary digression we can return to the question I started out with. What happens to employment and growth when rising labour productivity reduces the amount of labour needed to produce the pre-existing output and idles some of the workers previously employed? All would be well if the now higher incomes of the employed population would generate demand for additional material goods and the equipment needed to produce them in sufficient quantities for their manufacture to re-employ all the workers just idled. For in that case, employment would be undiminished; and the only effect of the rise in productivity would be the growth of output, real income and the stock of capital. That clearly is the ideal situation.

The necessary condition for that ideal situation to come about is well known from Keynesian economics. Intended saving must equal invest-ment, or intended extra saving must equal additional investment. But that simple Keynesian condition of employment equilibrium must be put a little differently now that we look deeper into the consumer's behaviour and realize that he divides his income not two ways, between spending and saving, but three ways, between spending on material goods, spending on positional goods, and saving. That raises the question: which two of these three uses of consumption should be bracketed together when stating the condition of employment equilibrium?

One's gut instinct might be to lump together the two kinds of spending and keep them separate from saving; but a moment's reflection shows that that will not do. It is clear that spending on material things elicits output, whose production generates employment and income. It is equally clear that the decision to save calls forth no output and so generates neither employment nor income. But why should the effects of spending on positional goods resemble those of saving rather than those of spending on material goods? That they do, follows from the fact that the supply of positional goods and services is limited and cannot be increased, or at least not very much.

If increased spending on positional goods and services cannot lead to the creation of additional input, it cannot generate employment either. What it does instead is to bid up prices until some of the previous owners of the existing stock of positional goods become willing to sell some of their holdings, and some of the previous users of the limited supply of positional services are crowded out by the price increase.

The producers of the services (and of additions to the stock of positional goods) enjoy an increase in rents, the previous owners of the positional goods that they are induced to sell enjoy capital gains and an increase in liquidity. The increase in rents is likely to stimulate spending on material goods, thereby indirectly generating at least some employment; but the main consequence of positional spending, the capital gains and increased liquidity of those selling some of their holdings of positional goods, is unlikely to do even that.

For the sellers of positional goods are typically the old rich. If they still are rich, their need for material comforts is well taken care of; and they will reinvest the proceeds of their sales in financial assets or other positional goods rather than spend even more on material goods. Those of the old rich who are impoverished and forced to sell some of their cherished and valuable possessions for that reason, are likely either to repay debt out of the proceeds, which is a form of saving, or to use them as a fund out of which to continue maintaining their accustomed level of living into the future, which again constitutes saving.

In short, additional demand for positional goods and services has almost the same economic impact (or lack of impact) as the hoarding of money, except that it also raises the prices of positional goods and shifts the distribution of wealth in favour of the affluent former holders of those goods.

That the demand for positional goods resembles the hoarding of money in its failure to stimulate the economy should come as no surprise. After all, to spend on positional goods is mostly to hoard art objects, antiques, first editions and real estate. Hoarding them and hoarding money or gold are very similar activities, because their objects are so similar. All of them are favoured repositories of wealth owing to their limited supply, which is either absolutely fixed or almost fixed in the sense that their existing stock is large in relation to the limited capacity of adding to it.

Keynes, as many economists before him, looked upon the hoarding of money as something akin to an anti-social act, because its limited supply keeps the demand for it from creating employment. To use Keynes's own words: 'Unemployment develops . . . because people want the moon; — men cannot be employed when the object of desire (i.e. money) is something which cannot be produced and the demand for which cannot be readily choked off'.[1] That argument has become well known and well established but was generally believed to apply only to money and gold. All I have done is to generalize it to include also the much broader and larger category of all tangible wealth that appeals to the wealthy along with a few services that also have a snob appeal. Thereby, I have shifted the sharp dividing line Keynes and others have drawn between money and all else to a new position where it separates money *and* positional goods and services from the material sector.

That dividing line, however, must be not only shifted but softened as well. For, as is usual with classifications in economics, the difference between positional and material goods and services is not as sharp and clear cut as I, in my desire to simplify the exposition, made it out to be. In reality, the borderline between them is quite fuzzy and gradual. To begin with, the increased rents of the suppliers of positional services and the artists and craftsmen who produce additions to the stock of positional goods do generate some secondary employment, as already mentioned. Second, many goods have both a material and a positional component. Third, excess demand for some positional goods degrades their quality, which often calls for additional labour or material inputs to prevent or offset their degradation. Finally, demand for such positional goods as made-to-measure clothes and the services of domestic servants clearly generates employment, although the demand for these is gradually being choked off by the rise in their costs, which accompanies the rise in labour productivity.

In its impact on output and employment, therefore, the demand for positional goods and services stands somewhere in between the hoarding of money and the demand for material goods and services, though perhaps closer to the former; and it differs from both in having a much greater impact on prices or costs — causing them to rise the more, the lesser its impact on output. I conclude, therefore, that the more advanced is an economy, and the larger the share of positional goods in its total spending,[2] the more will a rise in labour productivity depress employment and raise the prices and costs of positional goods.

Those are the bare bones of a mere theory. But how important is it, what evidence supports it, what are its wider implications and what are the remedial policies it calls for?

Statistics of spending on positional goods are as unavailable as statistics of intended saving — and for the same reason. The national accounts register spending only when it results in output, not when it merely increases rents or the turnover and market value of an accumulated stock of goods. Most positional spending, therefore, the part that elicits no output, does not enter the national accounts explicitly but is hidden as part of the residual item: personal saving. (One might say that national accountants, mindful of the national accounts' main function as a macroeconomic tool, have properly bracketed positional spending with saving and not with material spending.) Accordingly, the volume of spending on positional goods can only be gauged by piecing together data on current additions to their stock and the turnover of the existing stock — and by the indirect evidence of the rising prices of positional goods relative to the rise in the cost of living.

I cannot present comprehensive estimates, only a couple of examples. Annual sales of art objects and antiques in the United States are estimated at around $5 billion — a mere 3 per cent of personal saving. Much more important is our expenditure on upgrading, not the contents of our houses, but the houses themselves. Americans are known to be exceptionally mobile as measured by the frequency with which we move from one place to another in pursuit of a better job. But we are even more mobile and move house almost twice as often *within the same locality*, in pursuit of a better, more elegant house that presents a better image. Between 10 and 14 per cent of the owners of one-family houses move annually within the same town or county, which means a move every seven to ten years on average. In 1984 (the latest year for which data are available) 10.4 per cent of American homeowners changed house within the same vicinity, most of them (7.4 per cent) moving to a more expensive house than the one they left, presumably because their income had risen and enabled them to move to a house and location more appropriate to their new, higher station in life. Assuming that they paid, on average, 15 per cent more for the house they bought than the price they obtained for the one they sold, the total value of the houses they moved into can be put at $380 billion, with a net expenditure of $50 billion on improving that most visible and expensive symbol of their status. That is about one-third of total personal saving.[3]

I now come to the indirect evidence provided by the rising relative prices of art and housing. According to the Times–Sotheby index and its successor, the more reliable Sotheby index, the prices of paintings, art objects and antique furniture rose, in real terms (that is, corrected for the rise in the cost of living), by slightly over 10 per cent annually during the prosperous 1950s and 1960s, slowing to an annual 6 per cent rise during the past ten years.[4] For earlier times, an unpublished estimate puts the real rate of return on paintings at around 3.6 per cent for the nineteenth century and at 5.2 per cent for the beginning of the twentieth.[5]

Much the same picture emerges also from the American statistics on residential housing. Although housing construction kept pace with the growth of population and the number of families, housing prices nation-wide rose annually by almost two percentage points more than the consumer price index between 1918 and today. That figure, of course, is the average of the much faster increase in the market value of positionally favoured housing and the slower increase in that of housing not so favoured. (Indeed, a measure of the *dispersion* of housing prices, were it available, would be a better index of the value of the positional component in housing.) In climatically and culturally favoured San Francisco, the annual rise in the price of single-family houses was 4.7 per cent in real terms over the past 15 years.

Needless to add, the steady, secular, and fairly predictable rise in the relative prices of positional goods makes them good investments, which renders them all the more attractive as status symbols but also adds to their tendency to lower employment and impede growth. For not only does spending on positional goods divert income from spending on materials goods; the use of some of them as repositories of accumulated wealth also diverts funds from financial assets, thereby raising the cost of productive investments and slowing capital formation.

Let me now discuss some of the implications. My argument that, in too affluent an economy, rising labour productivity creates unemployment and slows growth reminds one of the stagnation thesis advanced half a century ago by Alvin Hansen. He based his argument on the belief that economic advance would gradually reduce opportunities for profitable investment, thereby reducing capital formation, depressing employment and slowing growth.[6] The profession has largely ignored Hansen's thesis, at first, because the long period of post-war prosperity made its gloomy prediction look premature, and later, during the period of stagnation, because it could explain the stagnation but not the accompanying inflation. My argument, that people's increasing affluence causes them to spend an ever-larger part of their income in ways that fail to generate employment and raises positional goods prices instead, is altogether different from Hansen's thesis, which it reinforces and improves upon.

For the rising prices of some positional goods and services, along with the worsening quality or increasing cost of others, exert an inflationary pressure on the whole price structure. Especially important and obvious is the inflationary influence of the rise in housing costs mentioned earlier; but Fred Hirsch discussed in some detail also the more subtle inflationary impact of the higher prices, costs, or debased quality of *all* positional goods and services.[7]

Accordingly, the increasing importance of positional goods and services in the consumer's budget has not only a *de*flationary effect on output, employment and incomes but at the same time also an *in*flationary effect on the general price level. In short, my argument is not a stagnation but a stagflation thesis. However, I am not presenting my stagflation thesis as anything more than one of many contributing causes of the severe unemployment and high inflation from which we have been suffering for the past decade, and for which the oil shocks of the 1970s and the preceding succession of bad harvests seem to be much more important explanations.

But, however much or little the thesis I am presenting contributes to explaining our past problems, it is a *systemic and chronic cause* of stagflation, whose importance is bound to grow with the growth of our affluence. Accordingly it should be useful also for identifying the long-run remedies of the chronic component of our economic problems.

I shall ignore, therefore, the short run and short-run policies, and focus on possible remedies of our long-run problems, which are long-run also in the sense of threatening to become more serious in the future than they are in the present. The principles of those remedies are simple enough to discuss here; I will not deal with the difficulties of their implementation.

If the argument I presented is valid, then one of the causes of stagflation is the discrepancy between the structure of effective demand and the structure of the availability of supply. Effective demand for material goods and services is insufficient, which causes unemployment and stagnation; effective demand for positional goods and services is excessive, which causes price increases and inflationary pressures.

That problem can be tackled from both the demand and the supply side. On the demand side, reducing inequalities of income would relieve both parts of the problem by simultaneously increasing effective demand in the material sector and diminishing it in the positional sector. For people at the low end of the income scale are far from having their demand for personal comforts saturated, even in the most affluent economies. Given more income, therefore, they would undoubtedly buy more material goods and services, thereby generating more output employment and income; whereas less income in the hands of the affluent would reduce their demand for positional goods and so ease the upward pressure on prices.

The correctness of such a policy is suggested if not proved by the Reagan administration's failure to stimulate the economy through its *opposite* policy of *increasing* inequalities. I have in mind the massive tax concessions given to business during the administration's first term, in the expectation that an increase in retained profits would increase investment and so stimulate the economy. What the increase in retained business profits has done instead is to increase the number of take-overs, which are the business world's equivalent of the consumer's spending on positional goods. As such, they raised share prices but failed to stimulate the economy.

The supply-side remedy would be to relieve unemployment by reducing the supply of labour and to relieve the upward pressure on prices in the positional sector by increasing the supply of social status; but only the first part of that two-pronged measure seems practicable at this stage.[8]

A reduction in the supply of labour is easier to think of as a reduction in the demand for employment. I have in mind to keep people, not from seeking employment, but from working for as long a workweek, workyear and span of workyears as they do today. That could greatly diminish unemployment at the cost of a small increase in the employed population's leisure, probably with benefits to both sides.

On a small scale and a strictly voluntary basis, the experiment has already been tried in the United States as well as in Europe, in the form of work-sharing and job-sharing — mostly to the satisfaction of employers and employees alike.[9]

A potentially serious problem connected with a shorter workweek is a psychological one. Our civilization trains everybody in the skills and discipline of work, but teaches only to a tiny privileged elite a taste for the constructive use of leisure and the skills and initiative needed to cater to that taste. That is why most people in our countries are at a loss and get seriously disturbed when they find themselves with more leisure on their hands than they are used to, and so know what to do with. Such disturbance usually takes quite a violet form in the young and energetic, exemplified by rowdyism and vandalism of the chronically unemployed youths who roam the streets of our large cities. Their behaviour is only partly an angry response to their rejection by society; partly it is also the normal reaction of boredom of energetic young people trained in the discipline and skills of work but left totally unprepared and untrained for leisure. In the aged, the same disturbance usually takes a non-violent but no less severe form, manifest in the disorientation and rapid mental and physical decline of those many retired people who are utterly unprepared for retirement, with not even a hobby or any other constructive activity to keep them busy and fill the emptiness of their suddenly increased free time.

Hopefully, however, the modest shortening of the workweek needed to reduce the chronic unemployment of our time would do more good than harm. The employed population could probably absorb an hour or two of extra leisure per week without ill effects; whereas the millions of jobs created for those presently unemployed would certainly do a lot of good, including the reduction of violence in our streets. In the United States, shortening by just one hour the 36-hour average workweek of an employed population of 110 million would create 3 million extra jobs; and even in the United Kingdom, 2 hours' extra leisure for 20 million employees would re-employ 1 million unemployed. The crude arithmetic of those examples may not be fully realistic; but it gives an idea of the orders of magnitude involved.

It would take a much more drastic reduction of the workweek to render acute the psychological problem just outlined; and in that case, the problem would have to be faced head on, probably requiring a major reform of our excessively work-orientated educational philosophy and school curriculum.[10] But that is not likely to be a problem in our time. Let me end this lecture, therefore, and acknowledge once again my debt for its main ideas to Fred Hirsch.

Notes

1. Cf. J.M. Keynes, *The General Theory of Employment, Interest and Money*, London, 1936, p. 235. Keynes, incidentally, also noted that 'land resembles money in that its elasticities of production and substitution may be very low' (ibid. p. 241); but as he was concerned with people's demand for liquidity rather than for status symbols, he drew very different conclusions from mine.
2. Note that economic and technical advance comprises the introduction both of new and better products (product innovation) and of superior methods of production (process innovation). The latter raise incomes and are likely to

increase the share of positional spending; the former are likely to increase spending on material goods. The two kinds of advance therefore are complementary in their macroeconomic effects.

3. All the data come from the 1986 *Statistical Abstract of the United States*. I have assumed that percentages referred to number of houses apply *pari passu* also to the value of the housing stock; and the 15 per cent difference in price between a house sold and the one bought by the same person is a rough guess.

4. The Sotheby Index of art objects and antiques is published weekly in *Barron's*, its detailed description in *Barron's*, 8 November 1981, pp. 4 ff. The now defunct Times–Sotheby index is described in G. Keen, *The Sale of Works of Art: A Study Based on the Times–Sotheby Index*, London, 1971. Unfortunately, there is a six-year gap (1969–75) between the latter's cut-off date and the former's base year.

5. For the source of those estimates and a short general survey of the economic data on the arts, see R.W. Goldsmith, *Comparative National Balance Sheets: A Study of Twenty Countries, 1688–1978*, Chicago, 1985, pp. 73–8.

6. Cf. Alvin H. Hansen, *Full Recovery of Stagnation?*, New York, 1938, Chapter 19; see also A.H. Hansen, 'Economic Progress and Population Growth', *American Economic Review*, vol. 29, 1939, Proceedings, pp. 1–15.

7. Cf. Fred Hirsch, *Social Limits to Growth*, Cambridge, MA, 1976, pp. 172–4. See also F. Hirsch, *The Political Economy of Inflation*, London, 1978, pp. 274–5.

8. The way to increase the supply of social status is to increase the ways or dimensions in which a person can excel over others. In our work- and money-orientated society, a person's income is the main dimension in which his status is measured; but in a more leisure-orientated society, which appreciates excellence in the performance of many activities, irrespective of whether or not they yield income, status would be measured in as many dimensions, with a corresponding increase in its supply.

9. Cf. Stanley D. Nollen, *New Work Schedules in Practice: Managing Time in a Changing Society*, New York, 1982; and the review and short summary of a report of the European Commission on the same subject in *The Economist*, 27 September 1986, p. 69.

10. Cf. R.F. Harrod, 'The possibility of economic satiety' in Committee for Economic Development, *Problems of U.S. Economic Development*, New York, 1958, pp. 73–4, for a succinct account of the problem and the difficulties of resolving it.

Index

achievement 113
see also motivation
active responsibility 82–5
see also economic responsibility
advertising 135
affluence 151–61
agents *see* decision agents
agriculture 11
allocative efficiency 11–12
see also efficiency
altruism 22
see also motivation
America *see* United States
antiques 157–8
anti-trust activities 83
Arrow-Debreu contracts 126, 130–1, 137
see also efficiency
assessment *see* market assessment

bad debts 20
Bagehot, Walter 20, 21, 80, 84
balance of payments
UK 33–5
US 61
banking systems 6–7, 10, 20, 83, 84, 142, 145
central banks 10, 20, 147, 149
commercial banks 134
credit systems 7, 20, 25, 131–2, 143
see also building societies
behaviour patterns 81–2, 112–13, 117–19, 121–2, 151–2
see also motivation
the Big Bang (1986) 8, 28
black market 78
see also economic responsibility
Black Monday (1987) 8
bond markets 129
see also markets
bootstrap situations 99
Bretton Woods system 9, 55, 56,
58–9, 60, 63, 73, 84, 142–3, 148
broadcasting policies 22
see also communications
building societies 27, 28–9
see also banking systems
Business Expansion Scheme (UK) 29

CAP (EC) 11
capital markets 133, 144, 145, 147–8
see also markets
central banks 10, 20, 147, 149
see also banking systems
Chicago school 76–7, 83, 98
China 35–6, 43–4
closed economies 56
see also open economies
closed shops 5
see also labour markets
collective goods 76–7
see also goods
commercial banks 134
see also banking systems
commodity markets 11–12
see also markets
Common Agricultural Policy *see* CAP (EC)
communications 54
see also broadcasting policies
communist economies 5, 36, 43–4
competition *see* market competition
complete markets 87–90
see also markets
conflict 111, 121
congruence 110–11, 112
consensus politics 22, 84–5
see also government policies
constitutional reforms 48
consumer price index *see* CPI
consumers 12, 39, 40, 49, 151–2
controlled disintegration 53–4
see also deregulation
converse theorem 109–10
corporation tax 30